T0326549

Douglas Gibson Unedited

On Editing Robertson Davies, Alice Munro, W.O. Mitchell, Mavis Gallant, Jack Hodgins, Alistair MacLeod, etc.

P.I.E. Peter Lang

Bruxelles · Bern · Berlin · Frankfurt am Main · New York · Oxford · Wien

Christine EVAIN

Douglas Gibson Unedited

On Editing Robertson Davies, Alice Munro, W.O. Mitchell, Mavis Gallant, Jack Hodgins, Alistair MacLeod, etc.

Cet ouvrage est publié avec le soutien financier de l'École Centrale de Nantes.

Cover Picture: Photo courtesy of Douglas Gibson.

© P.I.E. PETER LANG s.a.
Éditions scientifiques internationales
Brussels, 2007
1 avenue Maurice, B-1050 Brussels, Belgium
info@peterlang.com; www.peterlang.com

ISBN 978-90-5201-368-8
D/2007/5678/50
Printed in Germany

Bibliographic information published by "Die Deutsche Bibliothek"

"Die Deutsche Bibliothek" lists this publication in the "Deutsche Nationalbibliografie"; detailed bibliographic data is available in the Internet at <http://dnb.ddb.de>.

CIP available from the British Library, GB
and the Library of Congress, USA.

Contents

PART II. DOUGLAS GIBSON'S VIEWS ON THE INDUSTRY

Remerciements

Je tiens à remercier Douglas Gibson pour sa confiance, pour sa disponibilité et pour toute la passion de la littérature qu'il m'offre en partage.

Douglas Gibson m'a également donné l'immense plaisir de constater que notre travail sur cet ouvrage fût un plaisir réciproque, comme je l'ai découvert dans son dernier courrier avant la publication de l'ouvrage : « The book is shaping up embarrassingly well! »

Je tiens aussi à remercier Tom Becker pour ses encouragements et pour avoir trouvé le titre de cet ouvrage.

Avec toute ma reconnaissance donc à Douglas et à Tom,

Christine

Introduction to the Interview
with Douglas Gibson

This work compiled and written in 2007 is actually the result of a series of interviews which took place over a period of several years. Indeed, since the 1990s, I have followed Douglas Gibson's editorial work with particular interest. Our first interview, back in 1988, was a revelation: I was delighted to discover Gibson's passion and enthusiasm. When I conducted a series of interviews with industry players in 2005, I had the immense pleasure of interviewing Douglas Gibson again. This second interview, which is equally published here, focused not only on Douglas Gibson's career but also on his impression of the industry. As a follow-up to that interview, we decided on another project – which we accomplished in 2006 – revolving around Douglas Gibson's collaboration with "his" authors.

The purpose of this work is to create further academic interest in the files which Douglas Gibson entrusted to the McMaster University archives. Indeed, this interview throws light on the collaboration between Douglas Gibson and "his" authors – Robertson Davies, Alice Munro, W.O. Mitchell, Mavis Gallant, Jack Hodgins, Alistair MacLeod. The reader of this volume is given a flavour of what the archives reveal and is further invited to discover Gibson's correspondence and papers contained in the "Douglas Gibson Books" archives.

What this interview highlights is not only Douglas Gibson's outstanding editorial career, but also an exceptional depth found in his relationships and friendships with authors. Obviously, when one reads biographies and correspondences of editors such as Maxwell Perkins and Jack MacClelland, one is not surprised to discover close bonds between authors and their editors. The privilege of working with outstanding authors seems to require not only excellent editorial skills but perhaps subtler qualities as well – the capacity to nurture future talents by giving authors recognition and encouragement.

Douglas Gibson's experience points to as many different approaches as there are authors. For example, Douglas Gibson encourages Alice Munro to carry on writing short stories, at a time when she is systematically told that she will never be a great author unless she produces a novel. He is of infinite patience when dealing with Alistair MacLeod whose fine writing takes time. As an editor, Douglas Gibson adjusts to the rhythm and writing pattern of each individual author and goes so far as to suggest editorial tricks to help his authors optimize and promote their output. For example, he suggests a re-edition to Alistair MacLeod's *To Every Thing There Is A Season* in the form of a small illustrated Christmas volume. Or Gibson offers to regroup Mavis Gallant's short stories on the theme of exile under the title of *Home Truths*. And, in yet another example, he grabs hold of Jack Hodgins's lecture notes and asks the author to turn them into *A Passion for Narrative*.

These examples highlight the editor's double role: first, he must encourage the author's writing. Second – and equally important – he takes charge of the publication process and remains constantly alert to commercial opportunities.

The first role implies a permanent availability for the author when he or she requires support. And there is no standard recipe for this support. If an author seeks total independence, the editor will then allow for the author to have sufficient space. For example Alice Munro is extremely reluctant to discuss any forthcoming publication including her short stories. She will commit herself to a new volume only when the stories have been written and initially published in the *New Yorker*. Douglas Gibson must intuit the right time to suggest to Munro bringing the short stories together in the form of a volume.

Douglas Gibson's and W.O. Mitchell's collaboration is also crucial when the author reaches the stage of organizing a volume. Douglas Gibson gives a delightful account of their unique working sessions when all the short stories are spread out like cards on the hotel room bed. The Gibson-Alistair MacLeod relationship is yet again different. It is best illustrated by Douglas Gibson's reporting of a laconic conversation as a typical example of their friendly conversations.

The editor's simplicity in sharing his experience enables us to understand what is really at stake in the editing profession. Douglas Gibson reveals the subtle balance between literature, pragmatism, friendship, public relations and solitary work. The editor both organizes the authors' tours and protects their private space. He knows how to apply pressure on authors to write, and how to provide comfort when the pages refuse to be written. With both modesty and enthusiasm, Douglas Gibson shares his thrills and successes as well as his disappointments and failures. Among his most unusual successes, I would like to mention *Dickens of the Mounted*, the correspondence Charles Dickens's son. The volume is entirely compiled by Douglas Gibson – from the writing of the book (commissioned to Eric Nicol) to the illustrations (professionally arranged with calligraphic texts and a photo collection). In telling this story, Douglas Gibson delights in the trick played on the reader. To his great satisfaction, the book found its way onto the bestseller lists of both fiction and non-fiction, not to mention the *Encyclopedia of Canadian Literature* (edited by W.H. New) according to which *Dickens of the Mounted* is an unprecedented literary hoax, and Gibson, of course, is described as totally unrepentant.

However, hard work and dedication do not always result in immediate success. Some of Gibson's editorial difficulties include persuading Mavis Gallant to work on her Parisian Diaries. In spite of the success of *From the Fifteenth District* or *Home Truths*, the editor-author relationship is further complicated by geographical distances as broad as the Atlantic Ocean are at stake!

Whatever the difficulties and the ambitious objectives of Gibson's projects, what comes across in this volume of retrospections is the perseverance and the passion of each and every one involved. This is where the editor and the author truly meet – in this enthusiasm that Douglas Gibson shares when speaking about his collaboration with Alice Munro: "[I] delight at being along for the ride, as Alice's reputation just spreads and spreads!"

Finally, beyond the evocation of the personal author-editor relationships which are at the heart of this interview, Douglas Gibson gives us insight into two particular character traits which I enjoyed immensely in our discussions on editing. These traits – which Douglas Gibson obviously shares with previous generations of legendary editors – come as no surprise. These traits are simply the following: an incredibly mischievous sense of humour and, most importantly, an unwavering love for writing and for those who strive to serve literature.

Introduction à l'entretien
avec Douglas Gibson

Entrepris en 2007, ce travail fait suite à deux autres entretiens réalisés en l'espace de quelques années. En effet, depuis les années 1990, mon activité de recherche sur l'édition au Canada m'amène à suivre avec un intérêt tout particulier le travail éditorial de Douglas Gibson. Un premier entretien, en 1998, a été pour moi une découverte du dynamisme passionné de mon interlocuteur. Lorsque j'ai souhaité m'entretenir avec plusieurs personnes d'expérience sur l'industrie du livre en 2005, j'ai eu le plaisir d'interroger Douglas Gibson à nouveau. Ce deuxième entretien, également publié dans ce volume, a porté non seulement sur la carrière de Douglas Gibson mais également sur son point de vue sur l'industrie du livre. Suite à ce travail, nous nous sommes fixés pour objectif – réalisé en 2006 – un nouvel entretien axé sur la collaboration de Douglas Gibson avec « ses » auteurs.

Ce travail précède celui des universitaires qui se pencheront sur les archives de Douglas Gibson. Sans doute la démarche présentée ici a-t-elle pour objectif véritable d'éveiller l'intérêt pour une recherche méticuleuse à partir des dossiers légués par l'éditeur à l'université de McMaster. En effet, l'entretien retranscrit ici met en lumière la collaboration de Douglas Gibson avec « ses » auteurs – Robertson Davies, Alice Munro, W.O. Mitchell, Mavis Gallant, Jack Hodgins, Alistair MacLeod – et nous invite à découvrir la correspondance et les traces écrites contenues dans ces dossiers intitulés « Douglas Gibson Books ».

Ce qui est révélé à travers cet entretien avec Douglas Gibson est non seulement une travail éditorial hors pair mais également une qualité relationnelle auteur-éditeur qui se fonde sur l'amitié. Bien sûr, la lecture de biographies et de correspondances d'éditeurs comme celles de Maxwell Perkins et Jack MacClelland nous prépare à une telle découverte. Pour mériter le privilège de compter parmi « ses » auteurs des figures de renom, les qualités éditoriales s'accompagnent inévitablement de qualités humaines – une capacité à « nourrir » de futurs talents par la reconnaissance et l'encouragement. Douglas Gibson est l'illustration même de cette aptitude à l'écoute et à l'adaptation, et il nous révèle autant d'approches spécifiques que d'auteurs. Ainsi, il encourage Alice Munro à poursuivre l'écriture de ses nouvelles, à une époque où on semblait lui dire systématiquement, qu'elle ne compterait jamais à moins de produire un roman. Par ailleurs, il se montre patient envers Alistair MacLeod dont la qualité d'écriture demande du temps. Douglas Gibson s'adapte au rythme de l'écriture de chacun et propose également des astuces éditoriales afin d'optimiser ou de mettre en valeur leur production. C'est, par exemple, la réédition de *To Every Thing There Is A Season* de Alistair MacLeod dans un petit volume illustré et adapté au thème de Noël. C'est également l'idée de regrouper quelques-unes des nouvelles de Mavis Gallant traitant du thème de l'exil sous un seul et même titre, *Home Truths*, ou bien, encore, d'insuffler à Jack Hodgins le projet de mettre en forme son support de cours et d'en faire *A Passion for Narrative*.

Ces exemples montrent que si le rôle premier de l'éditeur est de soutenir le travail de l'auteur avec un infini respect de sa manière de produire, un deuxième rôle, tout aussi important, est de mettre en oeuvre des projets de publication et de veiller constamment aux possibilités commerciales de l'auteur.

Le rôle premier nécessite une entière disponibilité pour l'auteur dans l'élaboration de l'œuvre lorsque ce dernier cherche un appui. Et toute recette en la matière est bonne à être rejetée. L'accompagnement recherché par l'auteur peut se traduire par un besoin d'indépendance complète : l'éditeur se tient alors à distance. Prenons l'exemple de Alice Munro : celle-ci ne souhaite généralement pas qu'on mentionne son prochain recueil. En effet, elle ne s'engage sur un recueil que si les nouvelles sont déjà presque écrites – si le recueil découle indirectement, par exemple, des contributions au « New Yorker ». Il appartient ainsi à Douglas Gibson de guetter le moment opportun et de suggérer à Alice Munro de réunir ses nouvelles dans un nouveau recueil. Chez W.O. Mitchell, la nécessité de collaborer avec l'éditeur se manifeste le plus souvent au moment de l'agencement d'un recueil. Douglas Gibson relate des séances de travail dans une chambre d'hôtel où les nouvelles sont distribuées comme des cartes sur un lit qui fait office de table de travail. Chez Alistair MacLeod, la relation auteur-éditeur est illustrée par de fréquents échanges à la fois laconiques et drôles dont Douglas Gibson nous fournit un exemple dans cet entretien.

La simplicité avec laquelle l'éditeur nous fait part de ses expériences nous permet de comprendre les enjeux véritables du métier. Douglas Gibson nous donne à voir l'équilibre subtil qu'il s'agit de maintenir entre littérature et pragmatisme, amitié, relations publiques et travail. L'éditeur est aussi bien celui qui organise les séances de signature pour « ses » auteurs que celui qui protège leur sphère privée ; il est aussi bien celui qui pousse à écrire que celui qui réconforte généreusement lorsque les pages refusent de s'écrire. Avec modestie et enthousiasme, Douglas Gibson partage avec nous ses réussites autant que ses déceptions ou échecs. Parmi ses réussites les plus insolites, citons l'édition de l'ouvrage *Dickens of the Mounted* et qui reprend la correspondance de Dickens fils. De sa rédaction (confiée à Eric Nicol) à ses illustrations (lettres calligraphiées par un professionnel, assemblage de photos), l'ouvrage est entièrement élaboré par un Douglas Gibson jubilant à l'idée de jouer un bon tour au lecteur. Quelle n'est pas sa satisfaction lorsqu'il voit figurer cet ouvrage parmi les listes des best-sellers dans les catégories « fiction » et « non-fiction », sans parler de cette mention dans l'encyclopédie de littérature canadienne (éditée par W.H. New) selon laquelle *Dickens of the Mounted* est un canular inégalé !

Cependant, le succès n'est jamais acquis et, parmi les souvenirs de déceptions éditoriales que nous confie Douglas Gibson, il y a ses difficultés à convaincre Mavis Gallant de collaborer à l'édition de ses journaux de Paris. Malgré les réussites de *From the Fifteenth District* ou *Home Truths*, le relationnel éditeur-auteur est mis à rude épreuve lorsqu'il s'agit de gérer une distance géographique aussi importante que l'Océan Atlantique !

Quels que soient les difficultés et l'ambitieux objectif des divers chantiers, ce qui ressort de ce volume rétrospectif, c'est la persévérance et la passion de chacun : c'est là, précisément, où l'éditeur rejoint « ses » auteurs dans une exaltation que Douglas exprime au sujet de sa collaboration avec Alice Munro : « [I] delight at being along for the ride, as Alice's reputation just spreads and spreads! »

Enfin, au-delà des relations très personnalisées avec chacun des auteurs – qui font de cet entretien un véritable ravissement –, Douglas Gibson nous laisse percevoir deux traits qui lui sont propres et qui jalonnent également l'histoire des grands éditeurs. On pourrait sans doute les résumer ainsi : un humour espiègle et, surtout, un amour égal pour l'écriture et pour ceux qui la servent.

PART I

DOUGLAS GIBSON'S EDITORIAL WORK

On Editing Robertson Davies, Alice Munro, W.O. Mitchell, Mavis Gallant, etc.

C.E.   *In our last conversation, you commented briefly on your long-standing relationship with authors. I would like to focus exclusively on this subject in our present interview.*

You said, for example, that many authors followed you from Macmillan's to McClelland & Stewart (Robertson Davies, Alice Munro, Mavis Gallant, W.O. Mitchell, Jack Hodgins and Guy Vanderhaeghe).

Can we come back on these authors individually and can you tell us more about how you came to work with them and what your collaboration involved over the years?

Should we start with Robertson Davies?

Robertson Davies

D.G.   Yes, fine.

C.E.   *I remember you saying that Robertson Davies published* The Lyre of Orpheus *with Macmillan and then he came to you. How did that happen? How did your relationship move from there?*

D.G.   Yes, Robertson Davies published *The Lyre of Orpheus* with Macmillan and it did very well. So, you see, there is no magic in my being involved with Robertson Davies. But then two things happened: one was that I moved to M&S and two, Macmillan became a much less literary house, and they decided to cut back on their literary publishing. Consequently, authors in that category began to feel less settled there; and I was setting up my own operation at M&S and it was doing very well. So, as I recall, some years after *The Lyre of Orpheus*, Robertson Davies contacted me – we were in touch socially anyway, as you can tell by the letters published in *For Your Eye Alone*, which you mention in your questions here. One of the letters is about Margaret Drabble and I sent him a copy of the Margaret Drabble book, and Robertson Davies and I had been chatting and we had been visiting. And you'll notice that he very kindly ended his May 1987 letter with an enquiry as to the health of my wife – which is a side to Robertson Davies that most people don't know: he was a very kind man, a man you could talk to about family situations. So he and I continued to see each other as friends and former colleagues. And finally he had a new book and he or his agent approached me and said: "Look, there's a new book. Would you like to publish it?"

C.E.   *He had an agent?*

D.G.   Yes. His agent was a man based in New York... no, his agent *had been* a man based in New York but then he was taken on by Janet Irving (who is the wife of John Irving, the writer), and I think she was the one who approached me. But anyway, I was delighted to take *Murther and Walking Spirits* which was followed by *The Cunning Man* and so we reverted to our editor/author relationship, until his death.

C.E.   For Your Eye Alone *contains two letters addressed to you. The first is a very chatty, humorously-gossipy type of letter (dated May 29, 1987). The second (dated March 25, 1991) is equally warm but more professional. Robertson Davies responds to your editorial comments as he returns a typescript:*

> "Herewith the typescript of *Murther and Walking Spirits* which now embodies many of your suggestions and alterations. Not all, for I thought some of them needless, and some inadvisable, because I sense that your notion of the novel is different from mine; you have edited always for a rigorous clarity, and I feel that a certain fuzziness is essential to the nature of the book which is, after all, about a man whose perceptions are not those of ourselves (…)
>
> Here and there, my comments on your criticism are a little saucy – a protest against a too-literal reading. Do not take it personally (…).
>
> I welcome enquiries, protests, loud screams, or whatever.
>
> Rob. Davies"

Would you say this exemplifies your editorial work and your relationship with authors: you make a number of suggestions, expecting the author to take most of them into account, but not necessarily all of them? Do you remember what your response to this letter was?

D.G.   That letter is absolutely typical. You notice that there is a genuine debate there. Because my role is to ask questions and one of the questions was: "I think this is a little too unclear. Don't you think you should spell this out." And he said: "No, I want a certain fuzziness." This is a very good example of the editor doing his job, and the author doing his job. And that's fine. We are both aware there is fuzziness and that's fine. And you'll notice he complains and grumbles about my insisting on an insertion of an extra generation and that was because, to be unfair, he had young people escaping from the American revolution in 1780 and having children who were married in 1900 and that's an exaggeration but, clearly, it wasn't going to work. So he grumbled, but he did put in an extra generation and for anyone who stops to think about this – and I realize that the readership of the novel is only going to contain about 2-3% of people who actually worry about that sort of thing – but you want to be forearmed against the accusation of sloppiness. So we were both doing our job.

So, it's good you spotted that letter because it exemplifies my relationship with him and with authors in general.

What I teach young editors is that in the editor/author relationship, when both are working on the manuscript – the author has finished the manuscript and has offered it to the editor – the editor is then engaged in the collaborative process of being a helpful critic, outsider, commentator, reviewer, etc. In my case, I literally sprinkle my comments in the margins and if the author goes through these comments on the pages and says "no, no, no," that's fine. I haven't lost. If I say "Would you consider dropping this?" and he says "no," that's fine. It's absolutely pointless to start keeping score as to whether most of your comments are being taken on, that's beside the point. The point is you raise this question and let the author think about it. The interesting thing is that the most experienced and professional – and often that means the most recognized and accomplished – authors are the ones who react best to this process because they realize that what is going on is for a useful purpose: it's part of the writing process and it's giving them a second opinion, to use a medical term, that gives them a chance to fix something that perhaps they weren't totally happy with. That's the response I found that I usually got from the experienced and professional authors. The authors who are shocked and appalled at the fact that you have defaced their beautiful manuscript tend to be the younger, less experienced ones. They're sweating mightily to get this perfect...

C.E.   *They probably feel more vulnerable...*

D.G.   Exactly! But as their literary career develops, they realize that this exchange with the editor is part of the process.

C.E.   *They abandon this kind of take-it-or-leave-it attitude...*

D.G.   Yes, or this "Don't touch a hair of my baby's head!" Again, when I teach young editors, I teach that it's vital that they establish right from the start that "We're both on the same side here," and it's the side of the manuscript, so that it's as *good* as it possibly can be made. And I'm amazed when I look back at how confident I was – in my twenties – telling Robertson Davies this and that, and other authors as well. But they were, in some cases I would go so far as to say, grateful: somebody was treating their work so seriously and with so much dedication. And in almost every case, they appreciated that this was a professional contribution. So I somehow managed to succeed in getting this cooperative approach. And that's the key to an editor being successful in working with an author.

So yes, this exemplifies my relationship with him and with authors in general. I make a number of suggestions, and I hope the author is going to take most of them into account but I'm not going to be offended in any way if he doesn't follow any particular suggestion.

I've just had a very successful example of this, with a current author. He writes very well – it's non-fiction. But his epilogue somehow seemed all wrong: it was both defensive and aggressive. And I wrote one of those difficult letters saying: "We have bigger fish to fry here and what I suggest is that you scrap your epilogue and instead produce an epilogue that says: here are rules that apply in the world of etc. And you establish rules that will always apply in the world." And I'm happy to tell you that he said, you're right, and he's now done it very well.

This is a case where if the book had gone out with his original epilogue people would have said: "Oh he's just pleading his own case, he's so defensive! And who does he think he is? He claims that he got everything right." And now, this takes a whole different angle, and the reader says: "Yes, I see, these are general principles…" So, just in this past week, I've been successful in doing something which I think – to a considerable extent – is going to make the book a better-perceived book. And the author could easily have been outraged because I was interfering, but he wasn't. So I'm very pleased that this worked out.

C.E.   *Coming back to Robertson Davies, how much of your correspondence with Robertson Davies was left out of* For Your Eye Alone?

D.G.   Lots of it!

C.E.   *Yes, the two letters here give the impression of a regular exchange and yet there were only two letters.*

D.G.   Yes, I know. The editor of *For Your Eye Alone*, Judith Skelton Grant, was doing a wonderful selection of the best letters. But what I will say, though, is that when you write to someone like Robertson Davies, you tend to do your best work, because he's going to be a very witty correspondent. So I tend to put a lot into my correspondence, just as I tend to put a lot into my editing. So the two letters published are just the tip of the iceberg.

C.E.   *Do you think the full correspondence will be published some day?*

D.G.   I don't know. I doubt it. Because there were so many other influences that helped shape Robertson Davies's work. My role wasn't important enough, but who knows what directions future scholarship will take.

C.E.   The Quotable Robertson Davies *by James Channing Shaw was published ten years after Davies's death: was this marketing idea yours?*

D.G.   In the time between For Your Eye Alone and *The Quotable Robertson Davies*, there were a number of books. One of them is The Merry Heart, which I edited. For that book I did the overall introduction and then I did the individual introductions to the individual pieces. And I'm very proud of this because next year, Penguin is going to bring a paperback edition with much of that material and they are paying me for my introductions! As preparation for our interview today, I did re-read my introduction. It was written shortly after his death; there is an elegiac spirit to it and, definitely, the sense that I was preparing this book as a tribute to a great author and personality. And it doesn't read badly today. I'd done the same thing with Hugh MacLennan when I produced a book called Hugh MacLennan's Best. I wrote a short introduction and then explained my editorial role and then wrote a short introduction to each piece. That was very satisfying too. So, I've done it twice so far.

C.E.   *When did you publish these volumes?*

D.G.   *Hugh MacLennan's Best* was in 1991, I think… and *The Merry Heart* was published in 1997. As you know, *For Your Eye Alone* came out in two volumes: the later letters and then the earlier letters. It was shrewd marketing, although it didn't make a lot of chronological sense. So the first volume came out in 2000 and it contained a selection of letters written by Davies during the period starting in 1975 until 1993, just before his death. The second volume, *Discoveries*, came out in 2002. It starts in 1938 and covers the years until 1975[1]. And then *The Quotable Robertson Davies* came in, just by the happiest chance. James Channing Shaw is an academic, from the States originally, who contacted me five, six years ago and said: "Look, I admire immensely the work of Robertson Davies. I wonder about putting together an anthology." And I said: "Well, you have to get in touch with the family to see what they think. And then, when you've done that, I'll be glad to help." And he went away and contacted the family and I think it took some years for them to come around to the idea, at which point he came back

---

[1]   The letters in *Discoveries* touch on various subjects in Davies' life, including (but not limited to) the publication of the Samuel Marchbanks books, *The Salterton Trilogy*, the early days of Massey College, and *The Deptford Trilogy*. The letters in *For Your Eye Alone* include the publication of *The Cornish Trilogy*, *Murther and Walking Spirits*, *The Cunning Man*, and Davies' next novel, which was never published.

to me and said: "Here I am, I've contacted the family." And then I contacted the family directly – the family in this case was Brenda Davies (Robertson Davies's widow) and Jennifer Surridge (who is one of the Davies' daughters): they basically look after the literary side of the estate. So then, this was very easy. I published the volume. And it was purely by chance that it happened to be coming out ten years after his death.

C.E. *So you could market it properly ...*

D.G. As you know, I was away for a couple of months last fall for personal reasons, and so I missed the launch season, and I'm afraid *The Quotable Robertson Davies* was one of the books of the season that I missed. If I had been here, I would have been able to be helpfully involved in marketing it. But they had a very nice launch event at Massey College and Jane [my wife] went along and represented me and she said: "My husband, Doug Gibson, asked me to read this." And I had been very mischievous and after thanking various people my text included the line: "And to my wife Jane who is reading this I say: Peter Piper picked a peck of pickled pepper. And so on." And when I said I'd done this, my colleagues asked: "Will she really do this?" I knew that she would rise to the challenge. So that was a very good event.

The book, however, hasn't done as well as I hoped.

C.E. *It may do better soon, because of the up-and-coming conference on Robertson Davies at the University of Toronto that may revive interest.*

D.G. Yes. Maybe. What so often happens is when popular or prominent authors pass away, in the years immediately after their death their reputation somewhat declines, and it takes a while for interest to revive again. And I've seen this happen before.

C.E. *Robertson Davies has a public image which is very different from the one you describe. He is described as ... austere... maybe that's not the right word...*

D.G. Austere is good. I used to say he's like Jehovah...

C.E. *The long beard...*

D.G. But there was one remarkable incident... I should tell you first that I'm publishing an oral history of Robertson Davies. Val Ross – from the *Globe and Mail* – is going around interviewing people who knew him and building up a biographical picture of Davies. One of the memories I passed on to her, is of how I was a young editor, and I had the daunting task of introducing Robertson Davies as we launched one of his books – it may have been *World of Wonders*. And this was an event at the Art Gallery of Ontario and the main auditorium there held 400-500 people. And he and I were in an ante-room, a gallery where you could hear the buzz of the crowd waiting for us to come in and speak. I was walking around rather tensely and he was standing there looking God-like and composed. And in the course of my fidgeting, I happened to move past him and I heard him breathing in a shuddering sort of way. I turned and said: "Butterflies? Really?" and he said: "Yes, always!" And he looked the least nervous man you could imagine. So that was a great lesson to me. After that I thought: "Right, being nervous before a speech is normal! Even Robertson Davies is nervous! The trick is not to show it!" And it was a great gift to me.

And the other thing to consider – and we're in the realm of simplified psychology here – but if you're a shy person, what could be a better mask than to give a god-like impression? It encourages people to keep a respectful distance. And I think that was the case with Robertson Davies. He was actually a very kind man, someone I could discuss personal difficulties in total confidence, and he would dispense wisdom – he was a wise man. There are not many such people. (Pause) Now Alice Munro...

Alice Munro

D.G.   Yes, Alice Munro.

C.E.   *Alice Munro's biography came out a couple of months ago[2]. It contains the letter that Alice Munro wrote to Macmillan saying why she wanted to leave them and follow you to the Douglas Gibson imprint. This letter is definitely pro-Gibson.*

D.G.   I had never seen that letter until it appeared in the manuscript of this book... If anyone says to me now: "So, were you of any use in the world?," I can say: "Well, this letter says I encouraged Alice Munro so that she could go on writing short stories." Alice felt that she was under such terrible pressure to write a novel that it was blocking her creative output. I remember I said: "If you want to go on writing short stories like this, and nothing but short stories, to the end of your writing life, that's all right with me. You will never hear me use the word "novel." You will never hear me ask for a novel. I will never say: "do you think this could be expanded to a novel?" You keep doing this! That's fine. And I will go on publishing you." And that – which I don't think was a statement of genius but merely common sense – seems to have provided

---

[2]   Thacker, R. 2005. *Alice Munro: Writing Her Lives: A Biography.* Toronto: McClelland & Stewart.

Alice with great comfort and reassurance. We're all the better for it. So yes, that letter was so pro-Gibson that it made Gibson feel terrific! I suspected that a letter like that existed, in that I knew that Alice was working with Ginger Barber – that's her agent – to persuade Macmillan to drop the contract for the next book, which became *The Progress of Love* and let Alice bring it over to me. I knew that she had written to explain why she wanted to do that, but the first time I saw this letter was in this biography.

C.E.   *Is this what you found most moving in her autobiography in relation to your collaboration with her?*

D.G.   Yes, definitely! It's wonderful!

C.E.   *What gave you the confidence to encourage Alice Munro to carry on writing short stories? As a publisher, you are very much aware of the demands of the market, so what gave you that independence from the market to allow you to say that she didn't need to try writing a novel?*

D.G.   Two reasons: I thought the market was wrong. I thought that the statement "Oh, short stories don't sell" made no sense in a world where the same people saying: "Oh, short stories don't sell" are also saying: "People's attention spans are getting shorter." And I thought: maybe things will change. Maybe short stories are going to become more popular.

But that was 20% of it. The 80% was: look, Alice Munro is such a good writer, the world is going to catch up to her. All we have to do is keep publishing her. I thought she was badly served by her previous publishers who twisted *Lives of Girls and Women* into being a novel whereas, I think, if they had called it a collection of linked short stories, then reviewers would have said: "Well, it's almost a novel!" and would have done that work. But instead reviewers said: "I wonder if it's really a novel." So instead of getting the YES AND, it was a YES BUT response. And that's a terrible thing for a publisher to do to a book. Publishers are in the business of getting a YES AND response, and not a YES BUT. So I wouldn't have done that. I steer very carefully away from doing that, and I continue to steer away from that. For example, this fall, Alice has a collection of linked short stories called *The View from Castle Rock* which takes the true account of what happened in her family, from the days of the Scottish Borders in 1700 through the generations until they left for Canada in 1818 and settled here, and on through the generations until we come to her parents. And then we go from there to stories where the first-person narrator is a person like Alice Munro and the stories are reminiscences of what happened to her.

And these stories could easily be twisted into a non-fiction book. But I believe this would be terribly wrong because Alice in her introduction writes in effect: "The stories are based on true events but I've added scenes and dialogues, and things that simply never happened and I turned them into stories." And I said: "Yes, and when you do that, the book is fiction." A stupid person might have said: "My goodness, people are really interested in non-fiction nowadays. Let's turn this into non-fiction!" But here Alice Munro explains how the stories begin with non fiction and how she turned them into fiction, and it's a very interesting continuum and it's a very interesting collection of stories.

I'm looking for the YES AND response from reviewers: "It's so close to being something like history or autobiographies." If we promoted the book as non-fiction, we would be getting: "Well, how do we know that these scenes really happened?"

C.E.   Yes... *"Has she really done all the research?"*

D.G.   Yes, exactly that! So I'm aiming for the YES AND response and not the YES BUT.

C.E.   *How has your collaboration changed over the years, as she became such a major literary figure?*

D.G.   We deal in short-hand more. She knows how I will react to things. So, for example, I read, with rage, that she has accepted becoming a juror for the Giller prize this year, which means that her own book is automatically ruled out of contention. And I called her and said: "Why didn't you discuss it with me?" And she said: "Because I knew exactly what you would say!" and she just shrugged off my outrage.

C.E.   *That is incredibly generous of her to be a juror in this context!*

D.G.   It is! And it's infuriating too! And she ignored my protest! What I'm going to do is work very hard to make sure that, when the shortlist is announced, and at the award ceremony, there is far more outspoken recognition of her generosity. Because, you know, you can double your sales with the Giller!

C.E.   *Her last book won the Giller!*

D.G.   Yes! Anyway... So how has our collaboration changed over the years, as Alice became such a major figure? Well... over the years a larger part of my role has become protective. Alice has become more and more vulnerable to endless requests for interviews here and can-we-do-a-film-on-you there, etc., etc. If she were a different sort of person she could be traveling every week to read at an author festival or to give a speech. Everyone wants to give her an honorary degree and she refuses to do that sort of thing. And people get in touch with me and I say:

29

"Well, I'm sorry, she really doesn't do that." And they say: "Will you ask her?" and I say: "Yes, I will, but don't get your hopes too high." And then I ask Alice and she says no, and I get back to them and decline. So my role is protective and it's easier for her to say no to me than to them. You'll notice, I'm being totally honest in all this. I say: "I will put your offer before her. I don't think she will accept it. But I will do it." And I do. So I do a lot of "running interference" – this is an American football metaphor – and I didn't have do to that in the past. She was less reluctant to do publicity events, less reluctant to doing tours. But now she is. And indeed, now, part of the contractual agreement that we make is that I will not require her to go on radio or TV to promote her book. C'est la vie! And I have to explain it to all incoming publicists and marketing people and they ask: "Why is this?" and I say: "Sorry, this is Alice and that's the way it is for her." So that's a big change. Part of the reason why she finds these publicity tours and events so tiring is because she puts so much into them.

C.E.   *She puts so much into them?*

D.G.   Yes. For example, in the taxi between this TV studio and this radio studio, she's likely to become involved in the marital problems of the taxi driver. He's going to tell her stories and ask her advice. She's going to become completely engaged and think hard and worry about it, even later: "Do you think I gave him good advice?" So that's one. And the other reason is that she thinks her way through interviews in really concentrated thoughts rather than oh, yes!-here's-the-answer-I-always-give, and she's really tired at the end of it.

C.E.   *And it gets more and more time consuming as her fame grows. While we're on that subject, what do you think of Margaret Atwood's LongPen idea[3]?*

D.G.   Well, I wish it well, but I think it underestimates the importance of the personal contact between the reader and the author. You know, the she-is-smaller-than-you-think comments or she-said-well-good-luck… just that brief here-we-are and our-eyes-met moment, and I think that's why people line up. One of my roles is to hover protectively when, say Alice Munro is signing. So I'm standing there being polite but I'm acting as security, if you like, in case you run into a crazy person or – more frequently – someone who just keeps talking and talking, while there are fifty people waiting, and I simply have to say: "Excuse me, there are quite a few people here…"

---

[3]   Margaret Atwood has created a device she has called a LongPen, which allows her to meet and sign books for her fans all over the world from her own home.

C.E.   *Running interference?*

D.G.   Exactly. And I'm very good at it because I've been doing it for years. It's amazing how the appearance of an authority figure helps. I'm very polite: I don't say "Come on, move along!" I simply say: "There are quite a few people waiting, and I'm afraid..." dot dot dot. Or I can be more direct if necessary... but usually people say: "Yes, I'm sorry!"

What I have noticed is that accomplished and educated people line up for a long time to get to meet Alice Munro and when they're in front of her, they begin to babble: "Oh, I... I just wanted... I wanted to say..." and they're so excited. They've rehearsed what they want to say but it's flown out of their heads. And, Alice, of course, is terrific and she says: "Well now, what is the name? How do you want me to sign this?" and "How do you spell that?" and that gives them a chance to collect themselves. But the babbling happens so often! I'm used to it and Alice is used to it... And these people, I know, go away and say "This was so... so exciting! I..." It's very strange, because this is such an important meeting for the readers!

(Laughs)

C.E.   *So coming back to the way your collaboration with Alice Munro has changed over the years, you have become more protective of her. But what about the editorial side of things, are there any changes there?*

D.G.   I joke about that. Alice needs very little editorial help. Alice is such a self-editor. And in the case of many of the stories, they have already been through the New Yorker copy editing system, so no further changes are needed.

C.E.   *Most of Alice Munro's stories are published in the* New Yorker *first?*

D.G.   Yes, usually... But as it happens in this more recent book, I have been able to be more useful than usual because the opening chapter deals with the area of the Scottish Borders which I was able to visit and research, so I was able to give her the exact wording of inscriptions on tombstones. I was able to put some incidents from Scottish history into context. And I was able for example – because I think geographically – to tell her something she didn't know about the farmhouse of her great-great-great-...-great-grand-father in 1700. It was called Far-hope. It was called Far-hope because it was as distant a farm as you could get, going up from the North sea, up the river and if you come as far as you can up the Ettrick river, you come to the farm of Far-hope, and there's the watershed. Over the hill right behind the farm the water there is flowing to the West and into the Atlantic. And I said "Alice, do you realize that the farm was right on the spine of Scotland!" and she didn't know that.

The market town they went to was over the hill, and in another county, a Western county. She had visited but she didn't know the wider context.

So I was able to tell her this and I was able to explain how, in that part, you're very close to the English border and the English border still follows very close to Hadrian's Wall which is the border established by the Romans, and this is an area of Scottish history that I know very well. So you'll find that in the opening pages, I was able to contribute a lot. To my delight and honour, Alice has chosen to dedicate this new book to me!

C.E.   *That's wonderful! It is the first time that she has written something that involves so much research. So she probably appreciated your contribution.*

D.G.   Although, you remember, three or four books ago, she did a story called "A Wilderness Station" which is set in the 1830s-1840s in Ontario[4]. And there, it's the history of the area she grew up in. That required some research into the pioneer days. But *The View from Castle Rock* goes back many generations before that.

(Pause)

A week ago, to the minute, it was our sales conference and I told our sales people about this book. And I began by saying: "Alice has dedicated this book to me! So we have to do well with it!"

C.E.   *That's a good sales talk!*

(Laughs)

D.G.   Let me now jump over to the key point. My main role as editor with Alice is to say: "Alice, you've been polishing and polishing and polishing. It's perfect now! Please…"

C.E.   *"Let it go!"*

D.G.   "Let it go! Stop!" And this is a big joke between us because she'll phone and say: "Doug, I want to make just one change… Is it too late?" And I'll say: "Well, yes, but…" So it's a running joke and we've been doing this together for the last thirty years. So she knows I'm trying to stop her and she's always trying to slip changes in.

C.E.   *And she really doesn't need to…*

D.G.   Yes, and you know, I spoke about Robertson Davies. And Alice too is an immensely caring person and has known my family. I had a

---

[4]   "A Wilderness Station" was published in *Open Secrets*.

strong sense, when Jane [my second wife] and I became involved, that I had to ask Alice to check on her. So Alice approves of Jane.

(laughs)

C.E.   *Coming back to Alice's reluctance to let a story go without further changes, I remember Robertson Davies once said: "Always give it your second best... Never give it your best..." Or rather, I think it was one of his characters who said that... Yes, Eisengrim, in the* Deptford Trilogy*: "That was how I learned about never doing your damnedest; your next-to-damnedest was far better" ... "one should stop tinkering just before the play seems perfect." (*Deptford Trilogy *268)*

D.G.   Yes, that's interesting.

(Pause)

So, the main change in all this has been my delight at being along for the ride, as Alice's reputation just spreads and spreads. It just gives me pure pleasure. It's been a wonderful relationship. And every so often she says to interviewers that she's not going to write any more books and I don't comment on this. And then she writes more stories for the New Yorker. And then I say: "It seems to me you have just enough short stories for a collection." And she grudgingly admits that this is probably true. And I extract another book from her.

C.E.   *Do you think that's why she always prefers to send them to the New Yorker? Her stories can be published separately and she doesn't have to worry about collecting enough stories to publish a book?*

D.G.   Yes, that's right. That's it exactly. She never signs a contract saying "In three years from now, I will give you a collection of stories." She doesn't want that kind of pressure and so we just wait. And then, I say: "Oh, it seems to me we've got enough. We can now be planning a book for..." And then she might even use the expression: "I guess there's no getting out of it!" And then we'll deal with the contract.

W.O. Mitchell

C.E.   *What did you think of W.O. Mitchell's biography? It was written by Ormond Mitchell and Barbara Mitchell: you worked with both of them? What did this experience entail? What was your response to the fact that you are a character in that book?*

D.G.   The W.O. Mitchell biography was written by the husband and wife team of Ormond Mitchell and Barbara Mitchell, who are both friends. The biography was in two parts and the background story is interesting because when they brought the book to M&S, they deliberately chose to work with an editor who was *not* me because they said: "You're going to be a major figure in this and we think it's best to work with another editor." So I was proud to be the publisher of the book, and a very good editor named Jonathan Webb looked after it and worked with them. *Who Has Seen the Wind* – W.O. Mitchell's first book, and hugely successful – was published in 1947 and then W.O. Mitchell wrote many novels up until his death in 1998. So Ormond Mitchell and Barbara Mitchell had to cover a lot of territory and it took them a long time to do the research. By the time they were ready to publish, there had been a lot of changes at M&S. I had moved from my previous position of President back to doing just my own line at Douglas Gibson Books, and then the other thing was that, after that, Jonathan Webb had been let go in a reshuffle. So their editor was no longer there and they had published volume one and were asking: "What is to be done?" Somebody had to step in. And so I stepped in and said and "Obviously, Jonathan's not here and I'd be happy to help." So they overcame their understandable concerns about my being a character in the book and said, OK.

And thereafter, I dealt with them as if they were one. And how they divided the task is not clear to me, and I think with most collaborations it isn't clear – unless somebody is just the researcher and someone else is just the writer. Usually there's a mix, and it's more trouble trying to unscramble the omelette – for what purpose? I'm not sure how their collaboration worked but they *were* arm in arm. I had an ordinary editor-writer relationship with them, with this difference, that I was a character in the book. The other thing that I remember that comes up in my piece in the Quill & Quire is that they were very dedicated researchers. It was terrifying to see how much they knew about details that I'd long forgotten. As I say in my piece, they'd know that you had breakfast with W.O. Mitchell on such and such a date, and they expect you to know what you had for breakfast and to remember what you talked about. I found, as they researched – and they were brilliantly prepared – I spent much of my time saying: "I'm sorry, I don't remember the details." And it sounded evasive but I was being honest. The truth of the matter, is that the biographers are disappointed: "You spend your life editing W.O. Mitchell or Alice Munro and yet you don't remember…?," "No I don't…" On the other hand, the files tend to reveal things. And they say: "Don't you remember this?" And then it would come back to me. But at first, it's an embarrassment.

And that leads on to your later question about my files. In the future, those files are going to be almost useless because 90% of my stuff now is done by email. I am ridiculously old-fashioned and I didn't use to do the email stuff. I used to write letters and so there were files but now I send emails...

C.E.   *You would need to print out the emails, put them into the files...*

D.G.   Yes, and I should probably do more of that because I have been sending Douglas Gibson book files to researchers and there's going to be nothing from 2005 onwards because I've become an email person...

C.E.   *Do you value your correspondence with authors?*

D.G.   Greatly. Emails have changed the way I communicate. I think it's fair to say that I used to polish my letters much more than I polish my emails, and I say that with much regret.

I have donated my Douglas Gibson Books archives to McMaster University Archives. So it's nice to know that they are kept.

(Pause)

Well, anyway, coming back to the W.O. Mitchell biography, it seems to have done all right. After I wrote my piece there were no reviewers saying: "This book is much too kind to Douglas Gibson! But then what can you expect since he's publishing it!" It's fairly objective and obviously, I never got into discussions with the biographers as to whether they should be harsher or easier on me. I stayed away from those comments.

C.E.   *Moving on to Mavis Gallant and Jack Hodgins... They were among the writers who followed you when you switched to M&S. Has your relationship with these authors been fairly continuous over the years?*

Mavis Gallant

D.G.   Well, let's start with Mavis. A film was made about Mavis. I'm one of the half a dozen people in that film. Have you met Mavis in Paris?

C.E.   *No. I know that Margaret Atwood was meeting up with her a couple years ago when she was in Paris...*

D.G.   Yes, Margaret is also in that film and speaks very interestingly and intelligently about Mavis.

C.E.   *When did you first come into contact with Mavis Gallant?*

D.G.   Again I did something useful in my life because in the late 1970s (1977 or 1978), I wrote to her and said: "You are a Canadian writer, you write wonderful short stories and yet, you're not published in Canada. It's hard to get your work here. I think you need a Canadian publisher and I would like to be that publisher." And she wrote back saying: "What a wonderful idea! Yes! And, as it happens, I have a collection coming out quite soon. Maybe you can make arrangements to get the Canadian rights from my agent in New York." And I did. And the book was called *From the Fifteenth District*. I did a good job. I sent out lots of advance media copies to major Canadian commentators saying: "This writer is virtually unknown and I would like to change that..." And so we launched the book and I remember we sold over 4,000 copies which for a collection of short stories by a relatively unknown writer in Canada at that time, was amazing. I remember Jack McClelland bet me that we wouldn't sell 4,000 copies. He, a wise, creative publisher, just couldn't see how we could turn this Paris-based virtually unknown short-story writer into a Canadian success. And we did. And I never claimed the bet.

(laughs)

And then, everything that I'd hoped would happen, did in fact happen. And the reviews were all along the line of "Why isn't this woman better known? She's a wonderful writer, and we must claim her!" etc., etc. And suddenly her name was on everyone's lips, in the literary world. And the book did well in paperback, a year later.

C.E.   *Did she come over to promote it?*

D.G.   She did, she did. And I remember the launch at Massey College and the room was so crowded that people practically stood on counters. So yes, she did promote the book and it all worked.

C.E.   *You mentioned Massey College a number of times. Do you often launch the books at Massey college?*

D.G.   Well, it's just a coincidence that I happen to be mentioning that. All the authors that we discussed, except for Alice, have had Massey College launches. Robertson Davies became the Master of Massey College in 1963; W.O. Mitchell was writer in residence there for one year. For Mavis, I'm not exactly sure why we chose Massey college. But, yes it proved to be a good venue.

C.E.   *What were you going to say before I interrupted?*

D.G.   I was going to say that then I did something very intelligent. I wrote to Mavis in Paris and said: "Dear Mavis, you have written a book that you don't know about. Its title is *Home Truths* and it consists of the stories you've written over your career about Canadians at home and abroad. The main themes and characters are Canadians. And here is the proposed table of contents." And she wrote back saying: "This is a terrific idea. I would drop this, and add this... And then there is another story you didn't know about..." And then we dropped a couple and added three and that was it. We brought the book out. At my request, she wrote an introduction about what it was like to be an exiled Canadian writer. That piece was very thoughtful and very interesting. And the book won the Governor General's Award. And, from being the unknown author, she'd gone to the success of *From the Fifteenth District* and to winning the Governor General for *Home Truths*. Now sadly, she was not able to attend the ceremony which was in Winnipeg – the Governor General was from Winnipeg and liked to take events there. But Mavis had a broken ankle and couldn't travel, so I represented her. And I recall there was a fine Canadian moment because the order of these things is that the Governor General's Awards are given first to the French Language Children's Book and then the English Language Children's Books, and then, in pairs, you work up until it's the French Language Novel and the English Language Novel. And this was the early 1980s and separatism in Quebec was very hot. The winner of the French Language Award strode to the podium and proceeded to angrily denounce Canadian writing, Canada, Winnipeg, the audience, the Governor General and the Governor General's Award. And he finished by taking the cheque and angrily stuffing it into his pocket and striding off. This was all delivered in French. And the polite and unilingual Winnipeg audience gave him a terrific round of applause. And it was as rude as I'm telling you, it was a denunciation of all these things and yet he accepted the cheque!

C.E. *How incoherent can you get!*

D.G. And I, happily, in these circumstances, had prepared an acceptance speech and the first paragraph was in French. It was a graceful response...

C.E. *You prepared the speech? I thought you'd be reading something Mavis Gallant would have written?*

D.G. Yes, part of the speech was my explaining "If Mavis were here today, this is what she would have wanted to say..." But it so happened that, courteously, I also included a couple of paragraphs in French and that proved to be an important courtesy, in these particular circumstances. Sometimes things are well arranged.

C.E. *Yes! That was very appropriate!*

D.G. And so we did *Home Truths* and it was a huge success, it won the Award. And now she's a major author. Thereafter anytime we brought out a new collection of stories by Mavis, it was a huge success. She too was at Macmillan by contract and she chose to follow me to M&S. I was able to say to her agent: "Look, here's what I'm doing now.

Other authors have chosen to follow me and if at any point Mavis would like to come, I'd be delighted."

C.E.   *And so she did.*

D.G.   In the meantime, I'm working very hard to encourage her with her great project which is her Parisian diary. She's been keeping a diary for fifty years and I would like to do them decade by decade, by volume. I've suggested getting students in to help her with the typing because it's a painful job for her. I went to Paris to organize this! We had a lovely lunch. And then Jane excused herself and I said: "Mavis, what I'm here to propose is a way of helping you with the typing." And she accepted absolutely that, yes, help would be very useful. And I said: "I'm in Paris for two more days. I have this young person's phone number; when can I introduce her to you? Anytime tomorrow?" And then it became impossible for me to introduce the volunteer and it became impossible for this young person ever to meet Mavis. And Mavis said crossly, at one point, on the phone to this young person who was doing her best: "Oh, Doug thinks I'm going to die! I'm not going to die!" And you know, this woman is eighty-three and resisting help, although intellectually she accepts that, yes, it would be helpful.

C.E.   *It's a tough job...*

D.G.   It's a tough job and I'm failing miserably. I phone her and I say: "How are things going? How's the writing going?"; And it's one of the great failures of my publishing life because her diaries could be like the Samuel Pepys diaries. She such a noticing person, and she's kept these diaries over the years. And I can't get my hands on them.

C.E.   *I'd love to help you with this project. Nantes isn't far from Paris. I could be the next volunteer you would send over to help out with the typing!*

D.G.   Yes... What I said to her was: "Look, you've got them in hand-written form. This person would take the diaries and photocopy every page and you would then go through the process of editing anything private that you don't want. And she would type it etc." The theory is perfect, right? She can't deny the theory but she can deny any particular application. But let me keep working on her... But so far I'm failing.

(Pause)

So your question was: how do I carry on working with Mavis Gallant even though she is based in Paris? And the answer is very badly. I phone her, I write to her. When I get the opportunity – if I'm in Europe – I visit her. And I worry about her because she's old and she's become visibly frail. And I worry about her financial situation but I'm keen to solve that by bringing out the first volume of diaries and making her rich as well as famous.

C.E.   *Yes... I would love to be the next typist you send over to offer to help her.*

D.G.   Well, we'll wait and see. I'll keep working on her...

(Pause)

C.E.   *Let us not jump over Jack Hodgins...*

Jack Hodgins

D.G.   Jack Hodgins! Yes! Jack's first book was published in 1976: *Spit Delaney's Island.* It's a collection of stories set on Vancouver Island – you know people on islands are always different. He and I have worked together over the years, and published eight, nine, ten books, including a marvellous book for creative writers, called, *A Passion for Narrative.* The history there is that I knew that Jack was originally an English teacher in high school in Nanaimo, and then as his own literary fame grew, he was invited to teach classes on novels. And he became very good at that and taught at the University of British Columbia and, latterly, was on the faculty of the University of Victoria for fifteen years. I would sometimes be traveling out West, and he would ask me to speak to his class. And once, we were meeting for lunch before the class and he was just arranging his notes and I looked at them and said to him: "This is really good! Oh my goodness!" And so I spent months persuading him that people outside his class would benefit from his advice about how to be a writer of fiction. And, in the end, he did produce the book. And it has sold over 20,000 copies in Canada. And it's partly terrifying that there are 20,000 people who want to be fiction writers! But it's a great book! And Jack continues to write and has received a number of awards, as the Lieutenant Governor's Award for Literary Excellence for his contribution to writing in British Columbia, and he is a member of the Fellow Royal Society of Canada. He is a writer's writer. Other writers recognize him, although, to my sorrow, he never quite hit the jackpot. If *Broken Ground*, for example, had won the Giller Prize or the Governor General's Award, that would have been terrific but he won a Governor's Award back in the seventies when it had much less impact.

C.E.   *But he is so prolific and he comes awfully close to winning major awards. Doesn't that compensate somewhat for the lack of recent awards?*

D.G.   Maybe, but the way the game is played here in Canada now, the awards have become so prominent and successful that if you're not nominated for an award, suddenly nobody is interested any more. And *Broken Ground* was not nominated. And then he's written another novel called *Distance*, and another collection of short stories called *Damage Done by the Storm*, and I think he's excellent but a theory could be advanced that there is more interest now in East-coast writing than in West-coast writing. But you know, fashions come and go. And you know, in my role, I suggested a major historical novel that I hope he will consider – and you can tell, from *Broken Ground*, that he's very good at getting into history for his novels, so we'll see. And he reacted in a very Jack Hodgins manner and said: "Hum, lots to think about!" And I would have been appalled if he'd said: "Yes, yes!"

C.E.   *You edit a number of major short story writers (*Damage Done by the Storm *by Jack Hodgins,* Island *by Alistair MacLeod). Is your involvement any different from one form of fiction to another? Do you read the short stories when a volume is completed or as and when each story is finished? I imagine that writers have different expectations and needs?*

D.G.   As the editor of a short story collection, I have two main roles. One is to make sure that each individual short story is as successful a piece of writing as I can make it with my questions and so on. And the other one, perhaps more important if I'm dealing with a wonderful short story writer, is to make sure that the right stories appear in the right order – that the collection isn't thrown off by the inclusion of something that overbalances, or that the order is not wrong. Getting the short story collection in the right order is something that is more of an art than a science although you'll find in my Quill & Quire article, I shuffle horribly because the question was asked by the Mitchells why I put the stories in the order I did. And I remembered vividly how W.O. Mitchell actually physically ordered the stories: we were in his hotel room in Toronto and we dealt them like cards. "OK, this should be the beginning story, right, because it's strong and… and this end of the bed will be… and this is a light one and it should be followed by another light one… etc." and you know, it's a matter of shuffling and I recall with greatest pleasure that we had planned to devote most of the afternoon to doing this and we were done in twenty minutes, we were so much…

C.E.   *So much* en phase...

D.G.   *En phase* is perfect, because let me tell you another story to illustrate that. I was working with W.O. Mitchell on a book called *Trophies*. The working title was *Trophies*, as it dealt with an academic who had all the usual academic diplomas, but also he was a westerner and a hunter and he was determined to shoot a grizzly bear as a trophy. And he and his guide went to a remote mountain area called Daisy Creek and things got out of hand: the grizzly bear attacked him and clawed him and disfigured him terribly. But the guide managed to shoot him. The novel is about his recovery, physically and also mentally from this horrible experience, and also it's about the recovery from the death of his wife and lots of things are going on, including academic stuff. So *Trophies* was the title, and we were getting close to final decisions – you know, the point where you put the book in the catalogue – and I thought the title was all right but not terribly good. And Daisy Creek is such a memorable name of the place where this central terrible event took place and it all happened after Daisy Creek. So I went into our office and spoke to our sales people and I said: "What do you think… Instead of calling it *Trophies* we'll call it *After Daisy Creek*" and they said: "Yes, that's much more memorable." So I phoned the author and thought: this is going to be difficult to persuade the author to take my title. But I phoned to say the book needed a better title and W.O. Mitchell, a very excitable enthusiastic guy, said: "I agree, absolutely, I've got a much better title! I got the perfect title for you!" and I thought "Oh, no! I've got the perfect title for him. Now I'll have to talk him out of his title." But I was polite and said: "Alright, tell me your title!" and he said: "My title is *Since Daisy Creek!*" and I said: "Well, let me tell you what my title was: *After Daisy Creek*" and neither of us had discussed it before and we thought of it on the same morning!

C.E.   *That's a wonderful story! And in the end the title was indeed* Since Daisy Creek?

D.G.   Yes, I'm not going to take a cheap victory. Anyway, I think *Since* is better than *After*. But isn't that remarkable?

C.E.   *En phase!*

D.G.   Yes! As for the arrangement of the stories! Short story editing consists of getting the arc of the stories correct and that takes a lot of work but if it's an author you're in agreement with, it can get done quickly. And ideally, readers don't notice. They don't say: "What a clever order!" I think you only notice the order when something is wrong. So that's my main role and that's the chief characteristic of that form of fiction: you're dealing with small individual parts, whereas the novel you deal with as a whole.

C.E.   *Margaret Atwood used a similar metaphor for arranging poems. She said it was a lot like playing solitaire: you lay them all out on the floor and you arrange the poems in different orders and you shuffle them and re-shuffle them, until finally you arrive at the order that seems to make sense*[5]. *She uses that metaphor again in her poem "Playing Cards."*

D.G.   Yes. That's interesting.

(Pause)

D.G.   Coming back to your question about publishing a volume of short stories: Is my involvement any different from one form of fiction to another? Do I read the short stories when a volume is completed or as and when each story is finished? Do writers have different expectations and needs?

C.E.   *In the case of Alice, you've already answered that question.*

D.G.   Yes, it depends entirely on how the author chooses to work. I adapt. And this works for both fiction and non-fiction. Some authors say: "No, no, I want you to see this when I'm finished." Or "Well I want to get your response chapter by chapter." Again, an editor's role is to be supportive and helpful and for an editor to say "I don't want to see this yet," would not do.

C.E.   *But you could say that to new authors – I mean beginners? If they come to you with a couple of chapters of a couple of short stories, you say "Build it up to a full volume!"... Or maybe you're no longer in the situation where you consider submissions from new authors?*

D.G.   In the case of fiction, no. This doesn't mean I won't take on young authors but they won't be absolutely starting. Next spring, for example, I'm bringing out a book by a young author named Scott Gardiner (he's perhaps forty) and his book is called *King John of*

---

[5]   "Here's how you arrange a book of poems. You take all the poems that you think are worthy of inclusion and that seem to go together and you lay them all out on the floor... It sounds like playing solitaire. And it looks like playing solitaire, because then you start arranging the poems in different orders and you can go through them like a deck of cards, and shuffle them and re-shuffle them, until finally you arrive at the order that seems to you to feel right... It has an opening poem. And in that way, it is something like putting together the chapters of a novel except that with the chapters of a novel, you usually have some notion ahead of time what the story's going to be about; with a book of poetry, you often don't. So you put them together in an order that seems best to you. And it is obvious – and you can do this yourself. Take the book, and cut up the pages; lay them out on the floor. You know nothing about the table of contents; you know it changes it if you put different ones first. And that is just common sense, ordinary pattern working of any kind. You put the neck of the dress at the top, because that's where your head is. I don't know how it might be to have the neck coming out of one of the sleeves. You put an opening poem at the beginning, because that's where the beginning is. You put a closing poem at the end, because that's where the end is." Evain Christine, Khandpur Reena, eds. *Atwood on her work: "Poems open the doors. Novels are the corridors."* CRINI/CEC Canadensis series, Université de Nantes, 2006. pp. 100-101.

Canada, and it's a wonderful political satire set in the near future. He's written a book called *The Dominion of Wyley McFadden*. He's a fine satirist. And his new book is very interesting because it reflects the split between the American political parties between the red and the blue states. In Scott's satirical novel the split is so strong that they start getting serious about joining Canada. And then this amazing leader King John of Canada becomes immensely popular and then suddenly in the US it's becoming even more serious. So from the title on, it's amusing.

So that's a case of a new author coming to me. He came to me because it's clearly political and if requires a lot of shrewd knowledge of the political system here. And you know, I do lots of political books.

C.E.   *How did that author manage to reach you?*

D.G.   Well his agent contacted me and said: "I know you don't do many new novels but this is a political book…"

C.E.   *So, new submissions that you are likely to consider are invariably given to you by agents?*

D.G.   Yes. Or by authors directly. But you know, my contract at M&S requires me to do five to ten books a year and of course I do ten! So I'm working seven days a week… But I enjoy it very much. So I have enough writers… You know, Alice Munro published a book two years ago: there she is again, etc. So there really isn't that much space for more.

C.E.   *No, there isn't!*

(Pause)

D.G.   So to sum up my answer on your previous question, writers have different expectations and needs and I adapt.

C.E.   *Yes, you extract books from Alice Munro… Do you also extract books from Alistair MacLeod?*

D.G.   Yes, let's talk about Alistair MacLeod.

Alistair MacLeod

C.E.   *Alistair MacLeod is not a prolific writer but a wonderful writer; he takes his time to polish up his work. What was your role as he was working on* No Great Mischief *and* Island?

D.G.   There's a very good account of my role when he was working on *No Great Mischief* in the volume by Alistair MacLeod edited by Gilford. I wrote a ten-twelve page piece on how I encouraged Alistair, how I extracted the manuscript, and my role as an editor throughout the process. And that leads to *Island*. The answer is that he wasn't working on *Island* at all. And I use this as an example of the Alistair MacLeod dialogue. Everyone admires Alistair MacLeod but some people find his dialogue not as natural as they would wish, and my only response to them is they haven't listened to anyone talking to Alistair MacLeod.

Some weeks after *No Great Mischief*, I phoned him and we had a conversation something like this:

"Alistair, how many of your short stories do you have that have not been included in your two story collections?"

"Oh, there are two."

"And are they short or long?"

"Oh, they're both quite long."

"What are their titles?"

"One is called 'Island' and the other is called 'Clearances.'"

"Well, I think in the spring we will publish a book called either *Island* or *Clearances*. And it will include those two stories plus the other stories and it will be subtitled *The Collected Stories of Alistair MacLeod*. And I think it will do very well."

"Do you think so?"

"Yes, I do. And I have been right before." And we both laughed.

And that's exactly what happened.

And the book has been hugely successful. By buying *No Great Mischief* and *Island*, people had the complete work of Alistair MacLeod.

So that was my role: he had written *Island* without knowing it!

C.E. *And who came up with the idea to do the Christmas book* To Every Thing There Is A Season: A Cape Breton Christmas Story *by Alistair MacLeod (with illustrations by Peter Rankin)?*

D.G.   Well I asked Alistair whether he had a new story. And he said no, I don't. So I said: "Here's what I plan to do. We'll make a short Christmas book out of *To Every Thing There Is A Season*. And I will get an illustrator to make it work." I found Peter Rankin as an illustrator, and I didn't realize before I signed him up that he was actually a third-cousin of Alistair's. So that was wonderful. And then my role there was very interesting because I worked hard with our sales people to decide what the ideal size for this little Christmas book was. So we came up with that. And I then went up to our designers and said: "Here is the short story *To Every Thing There Is A Season*. Let's work on a design that fits this page." So they came up with a sample page. I said: "Alright, using that, run out the whole story and tell me how many pages you have." It turned out to be only 18 pages. So, I had a considerable job. You'll find that the book contains an introduction, written by me. And at the end of the book, there's quite a lot about Alistair MacLeod and quite a lot about the illustrator. Having done that, I worked with the illustrator. I marked the text with comments: "Maybe an illustration of the cows here... or of the horse here..." – marking all the possible illustrations. And then he would do rough drawings and then I would say "That should be a full page...That should be a half-page..." And we wanted everything to fall into place perfectly. So the illustrator went away and did half-pages and full pages, etc. And in it all came, along with the title page and everything. And I was hovering as the designer was trying to put everything into place, and it wasn't working! Nothing was the way we had planned it. We had two pages of just text and then too many illustrations. And it was six thirty, so I said: "All right, let's try tomorrow." Now, at four o'clock in the morning, I thought: "The cows! We're missing the cows!" And then, when the office opened, I phoned in, and the designer said: "Yes, you're right, *somewhere* we lost the illustration of the cows!" And we put that in and everything fell into place." So this has now become a joke in the office: "The cows! The cows! We're missing the cows!"

And the book has been a huge success. Many people who buy it I'm sure have *Island*, but they want this as a Christmas present. And we're going to bring it out every Christmas...

C.E.   *So that was a great idea...*

D.G.   And if Alistair isn't writing new books then I will invent new books for the Alistair MacLeod market.

C.E.   *You do that to keep the Alistair MacLeod market continuously interested?*

D.G.   Yes, yes! And I've said to Alistair, any time you finish a short story, let me know. I can do magic with it. But I wrote to him recently and said: "It's been a long time now. And I know it takes time. And I know you've been busy traveling the world. But maybe it's time to stop. Maybe it's time to become a writer again."

C.E.   *You do want him to know that you're very eager to publish more of his stories.*

D.G.   Yes.

C.E.   *How much do the above writers tell you about their work-in-progress? Do you put any pressure on them to keep you posted?*

D.G.   Some do, some don't. It's up to me to be in constant friendly contact. And I will say: "So, how's the writing going?" And some of them are happy talking about it and some are not. Nobody is going to be offended that their publisher is expressing a friendly interest. Although, as I said, with Mavis, distances do make things difficult.

C.E.   *Before we leave the subject of publishing fiction to move on to non-fiction, can you tell me a little bit about Guy Vanderhaeghe?*

Guy Vanderhaeghe

D.G.   Yes, I have been the publisher for all of Guy's work but I've never been his editor. So I was a publisher at Macmillan when he wrote a shy letter asking me whether I'd be interested in his stories. And it worked the way the system is supposed to work. Our readers came back and said: "This man is great!" I remember I was actually ill with flu and I read his stories in bed and then came back to the office and said: "You're right! This man is great!" And that was his book *Man Descending* which won the Governor General's Award – his first collection of stories.

And since then he wrote a number of novels and collections of short stories and he always gets better and better. I think you may have noticed that the French edition came out recently and it got wonderful reviews. Mavis Gallant sent me a copy. She maintains a sort of motherly interest in Canadian writers.

My role with Guy was one of constant encouragement. And he was with me at Macmillan and then I like to think that he followed me at M&S, but the timing was such between his books that by the time he arrived I was no longer just doing the Douglas Gibson Books – as I was from 1986 to 1988 – but doing the whole publisher thing. So I was glad to help attract him to M&S and glad to see him taken on by Ellen Seligman, and they have both worked together very happily on a number of super books.

Donald Jack

C.E.   *Now, Donald Jack?*

D.G.   Donald Jack came to me with *That's Me in the Middle* which was the winner of the 1974 Stephen Leacock Award. That was part of a series...

C.E.   *Apparently, there are eight volumes?*

D.G.   Yes, that's right: *The Bandy Papers* which recount the adventures of Bartholomew Bandy, a World War I fighter pilot – very humourous. But we have stopped publishing them, and sadly the author has passed away and we're letting the books go out of print. As we brought out the later books, we found that the market was dying away.

C.E.   *How did Donald Jack first approach you?*

D.G.   The history there is that he brought out the first book in 1962, and it did very well. Then he disappeared. He got in touch with me in 1969 and said: "I wrote this book in 1962 and I've now written a continuation of it. It's the same character and it's called *That's Me in the Middle*." And I liked it very much and said: "We're going to take both books so that the end of Volume One becomes the beginning of Volume Two, and we will publish the two together and make it part of a series!" And so we did and it was hugely successful at first. That was at Doubleday Canada. And Doubleday continued to publish the series – up to seven volumes. And then Donald Jack came to me with his last one, *Hitler Versus Me*, and I published it with great affection. He was at work on a final volume, *Stalin Versus Me*, but he passed away. With my encouragement, the series has been adopted by a young publisher in New Brunswick and he's supplied an ending for *Stalin Versus Me*. The rights for the other books are now his. So the books will continue to live, and that's the main thing.

(pause)

D.G.   The other author I haven't mentioned is William Weintraub.

William Weintraub

D.G.   Bill is eighty years old, and he writes light and funny books. I was delighted to publish him last fall, when he wrote a coming of age novel, called *Crazy About Lili*. It's set in 1948. It's about an 18-year-old McGill student who desperately wants to lose his virginity and ends up falling in love with a stripper. Now Bill is at work on continuing the career of our young hero whose career is very close to the author's. Just as Bill made a living as a young writer traveling in Europe, I think that our hero is about to do that. So we'll see.

Non-fiction Authors

C.E.   *Your list of non-fiction authors is equally impressive. Can you tell us about your experience with each one of them?*

D.G.   No! We would be here for the rest of the year!

C.E.   *Your imprint continues to represent your personal interests (as stated on the web pages, these interests are eclectic – fine fiction, history, public affairs, humour, the great outdoors, the sea, the Rockies and the adventures of risk-taking travellers).*

D.G.   Yes, you will notice I have a weakness for a number of things... I've added something to that list. Just in this past week, I thought "I'm really interested in Quebec," so it's now on the list. And yes, it's lovely to be able to say, I have a weakness for all of these areas. These are the sort of books I want to do!

C.E.   *How do you determine the sort of balance you're looking for, for your imprint?*

D.G.   I don't want to take on more than 2-3 books of fiction a year, because I want to keep the fiction list small and distinctive. So for instance this fall is Alice Munro, and the first volume of the series about Montreal by Yves Beauchemin which is *à la Balzac*, because the book makes Montreal the hero although we do follow the adventures of an individual. I'm engaged in trying to break down the two solitudes by getting English authors to say: "This is an important writer; what he's telling us about this mysterious world is important."

So the question of balance is interesting. I'm falling down at the moment on my balance in books of adventure – I've one nice sea-faring story coming out this winter: *Sailing Away from Winter* by Silver Donald Cameron.

As it happens, this year I'm very heavy on serious political books. I published one book last summer called *Stephen Harper and the Future of Canada* by William Johnson which did well. When we brought it out, most people didn't think Harper was going anywhere. And it proved to be a work of genius because Stephen Harper is now our Prime Minister. So the author is in the process of updating it now. And then I've got another book, which is being written as we speak, about the topsy-turvy events in the last five years in Canada where Paul Martin has gone from being popular to being thrown out. And then I've also got a book on language policy called *Sorry, I Don't Speak French* by Graham Fraser – a highly political issue. And I'm also at work on the Mulroney Memoirs. And I'm also doing a book by Jean Chretien's personal assistant, a man named Eddie Goldenberg, on the way it works in government.

Someone recently asked me: "Is your office in Ottawa?" and I said: "No, no, no. I do other books too!"

(Laughs)

One major addition to my list here is a book about a Canadian businessman. It's such a successful business story that it comes into the realm of public affairs. This man is Frank Stronach. His company is worth twenty-five billion dollars. In Austria, he's such a huge figure that a satirist recently wrote a book based on the supposition that he'd bought the entire country.

C.E.   *What is the sort of political books you are likely to accept?*

D.G.   Political books from any part of the spectrum. I was happy to be Trudeau's editor. I'm happy to be Brian Mulroney's editor. And I've published people from every major party. My role is clearly expressed: I'm there to help all participants in making their case and thus enlivening the public debate. This has involved a major surprise in the book we're about to launch in about three weeks which is the new biography of the Young Trudeau by friends of his named Max and Monique Nemni who discovered that, until 1944, when he went to Harvard and Trudeau was twenty-five – and this was a terrible shock to them – that he was an anti-semite, and pro-fascist. And his great heroes were Pétain, and Mussolini, and Degrelle. Do you know Léon Degrelle, the Belgium fascist? Degrelle wrote terrible fascist things. And we know Trudeau read him and admired him because he kept notes on everything he read.

The Young Trudeau biography came out in French about a month ago and it exploded. And we managed to bring in the English translation. It's called *Young Trudeau.* And I know people will say: "How could you do this to him?" And I'll say: "He did this to himself in that he invited the authors to go through the archives."

C.E.   *Does the book show how Trudeau moved on from this position?*

D.G.   Yes, and, as I wrote on the back of the book, it shows how far he had to go to become the Prime Minister he became.

C.E.   *Do the political books ever end up disappointing you? I remember you saying that Sheila Copps's book was very controversial but was actually less accurate than you would have wished. That was something that came out after the publication of* Worth Fighting For.

D.G.   Yes, we took a lot of heat with Sheila Copps's book. People said: "She's wrong here," and we weren't able to prove that she was right. She was facing a fair amount of disbelief. It remains a possibility that some of the things she said were wrong. Anyway, we lost a battle in the court of public opinion and that's always disappointing.

C.E.   *What about other controversial books such as* Stephen Harper and the Future of Canada *or Peter C. Newman's* Here Be Dragons.

D.G.   Any political book is likely to be controversial because people feel strongly about politics. We haven't had criticism about William Johnson's *Stephen Harper and the Future of Canada*. Peter C. Newman's *Here Be Dragons* is his biography so there has been criticism: "Oh, I'm not sure this happened this way!" but over all it's held up pretty well.

C.E.   *Do you often turn books down?*

D.G.   Yes, all the time. If you're in the business of publishing, you reject far more than you accept. If you walk into a room full of writers, it is an act of considerable courage because I know that in every group I run into, there's going to be someone I turned down. When I speak to young people in publishing, I say: "To govern is to choose. To publish is to choose. When you choose, you upset far more people than the few you make happy." Recently, since I've reverted to just working on Douglas Gibson Books, I sometimes respond: "I'm sorry this is a fine piece that can be published and I'm sure someone else will do well with it, but it's not right for me."

C.E.   *Do you have someone who helps you with the selection?*

Yes. Trena White is my assistant which is roughly a half-time job for her because she's a young bright editorial person in M&S. And she's helping me right now for example. We were working this morning and I said: "Look, this manuscript which is now ready to go to typesetting has been changed quite a bit and there are a lot of scribbled-in changes by the author. Could you please go through and see which pages are so written over that they are unclear and deserve to be re-typed." She's looking after that. And I suspect that she will recommend that ten or twelve pages be re-typed. That's the sort of support she can give me on a specific manuscript. And then if I say to her I've decided to do this book and I've reached an agreement with the author or agent, she helps me with the in-house procedures, she fills in the forms and prepares the contract.

C.E.   *In your last interview with me you said: "The difference between editing fiction and non-fiction is that in non-fiction, a good editor has to approach the book, to some extent, in the manner of a prosecuting attorney who asks questions: 'Can you prove this?' 'But how can you say this?' He has to attack the thesis and make sure that it stands up... So he approaches it in an almost hostile fashion to be sure that what remains after all the punching is solid." Can you choose examples from your past experiences with non-fiction authors and tell me about your prosecutorial approach?*

D.G.   I'll give you one very good story of the prosecutorial approach. Let's see if I can dig the book out for you.

(D.G. hands C.E. a copy of the book)

The book is called *Dual Allegiance* by Ben Dunkelman. Ben Dunkelman grew up in Toronto, fought in the Second World War, and had "a very good war." He was decorated with the DSO and he was a hero to his men, and to his country. After the war Dunkelman comes back to Toronto and he starts working in the family factory, a large factory called Tip Top Tailors, and the family is a distinguished, prominent Jewish family. And then the State of Israel is created and attacked from all sides and Ben smuggles himself in and says: "Could you use a Canadian major who knows about artillery," and he ends up in charge of the Israeli army in the North. This is the man who's establishing the border with Lebanon and he's hugely successful but when Israel is established, he goes back home to live peacefully in Toronto...

C.E.   *to run the family business?*

D.G.   Yes. He comes back to run the family business. This story was so unbelievable that in my role – prosecutorial role – I said: "Ben, I believe you but, you know, your role in this war is so extraordinary, is there anyone you could get to back it up?" He said: "Would Rabin do?" I said: "I'm sorry?" he said: "Rabin... Prime Minister Rabin of Israel. We fought together." And I said: "That would be OK..." He was such a modest man that he really did say: "Would Rabin do?"

C.E.   *And you really did say: "I'm sorry?"*

D.G.   Yes! So there's a prosecutorial story! What I said was: "This is an extraordinary story, and can you help me... if anyone is a doubter..."

C.E.   *And he actually wrote the story himself? Or did he get a ghost writer to write it?*

D.G.   He got a ghost writer to write it and I was involved too. But it's a lovely story. *Dual Allegiance.*

C.E.   *Are you involved in the practical details of getting a ghost writer?*

D.G.   I can be sometimes. I was not in that case. I always urge authors to try to do the writing themselves, because it's going to be more personal and much better, even if it means that they'll have to do more work. Some of them start and then say: "I'm sorry... I need someone to help me write this..."

C.E.   *What are other striking non-fiction editing experiences you may want to tell me about? The following list of authors may serve to prompt you: John Sawatsky, Andy Russell, Barry Broadfoot, Myrna Kostash, Harold Horwood, Don Starkell (author of the classic* Paddle to the Amazon*), James Houston (*Memoirs of an Igloo Dweller, *and other titles) and Peter Gzowski (*The Private Voice, *and other titles).*

D.G.   Let me just run though these authors very briefly.

John Sawatsky

D.G.   John Sawatsky was an Ottawa-based man, now based in the US, who was very shrewd. He wrote a book about a Soviet spy who helped create the cold war. John is a very precise researcher. His book was called *The Insiders: Government, Business & the Lobbyists.* John required very little prosecutorial approach from me because he was proving everything as he went along. So he's a model author in that way.

Andy Russell

D.G.   Andy Russell died just a year ago. He was a wonderful old Stetson-wearing westerner who wrote an autobiography called *Memoirs of a Mountain Man.* I stayed with him several times at his ranch and found that we could see grizzlies there. I once saw four grizzlies.

He was a great story-teller and yarner so my job as an editor was to turn him loose and often supply background for people who were not mountain men or cowboys or trail guides. But because Andy was a mountain man and storyteller, he wasn't going to run into the same the sort of questioning that John Sawatsky was.

Barry Broadfoot

D.G.   Barry Broadfoot is a most interesting case. He went around with a tape recorder – like yourself. And he collected these individual stories and he sent them in on to me in apple cartons – hundreds of thousands of words. And I would read them. The usual ratio that I took was about one to forty. He would give me forty pages and I would say: "Yes, that one paragraph, I'll take that." And I took over the whole front room of our house – again like Margaret Atwood – and I said: "Stories of the children over here, stories from the farm in this corner, stories about harsh employment here, …" And I would shuffle them and find that I had too much for this chapter, not enough there, etc. The book, *Ten Lost Years*, became such a success that the Depression is now known as "the ten lost years." *Ten Lost Years* became a play, which went to the Edinburgh Festival and travelled all over Canada… So my role there was to pull out these stories – they were all first-person narrative.

So that was one of the most rewarding books that I ever published because we were inventing the form, as we went. We decided to keep the stories anonymous. We decided to group them in chapters by subject matter. One speaker may have five different stories appearing in five different chapters…The cumulative effect of these hundreds of voices and stories is so powerful, it really is a great piece of democracy. It provides us with voices of ordinary people remembering what the Depression was like. And it led to *Six War Years* – people in the war years remembering what the war was like, at home and abroad.

And it led to a brief career for me as an authority on oral history. When the oral history academics held a conference, I was invited to speak, and talked about the rules we had established for this book. Tape recorders were relatively new then. And Barry was a most extraordinary case. He had been the literary editor with the *Vancouver Sun* and he had been briefly an infantryman in the Second World War. He was a newspaper-man for twenty years and he kept saying: "I'm going to write a book some day." And then one day, in 1970 he simply walked into his office and said: "I'm quitting!" They thought he was drunk: "Are you seri-ous?," "Yeah! I'm going to write a book. I'm going to take a car and cross the country and interview people." And he did. And he came to Toronto and got in touch with me because I'd known him on my travels as an editor. We were having lunch, and I said: "What have you been doing?" and he said: "Look at this!" and he pulled out the tape recorder and a bunch of interviews on paper. "I go round and I talk to people and I get all of this on tape. I'm taking them to Jack McClelland on Mon-day." And I said: "Can I take these back?" He never got to see McClelland because I said: "Give me your phone number... We can do this!" And it was a wonderful book. That came out in 1973. It was such a huge success and people thought: "Who is this young editor who is creating this thing with this author and this tape recorder?" I owe this project a lot for drawing attention to me and shortly afterwards, I was taken from Doubleday to Macmillan. In fact, I was in the middle of editing his next book, *Six War Years*, and I said: "No, I have to finish editing this!"

So that's Barry Broadfoot. All these years later, I have *Ten Lost Years* still in print at Douglas Gibson Books.

Myrna Kostash

D.G.   Myrna Kostash is a fine writer from the West. She wrote about different people. That was an easy editorial process. She wrote: *No Kidding The Next Canada In Search of Our Future Nation.*

Harold Horwood

D.G.   Harold Horwood, who died last year, was a wonderful naturalist writer. And he wrote such beautiful prose. My role was to shuffle his chapters rather than to do anything major.

Don Starkell

D.G.   Don Starkell did the paddling and wrote the original diary but a fine writer named Charles Wilkins did the editing and linking for *Paddle to the Amazon.*

James Houston

D.G.   You're in a little shrine of James Houston because he went to the North and as you can see (Douglas Gibson point to the paintings in his living room), he was a great artist. These are from the 1940s...

These are his memoirs: *Confessions of an Igloo Dweller,* etc. And this September, I have the huge honour of going on a cruise around the Arctic. It's a James Houston memorial cruise – because I was his editor, I have been asked to go along free, as a resource person...

James Houston had a huge influence on me. You know I spoke at his funeral in Connecticut, and I wrote a long piece for the Toronto Star – an appreciation of James Houston.

Peter Gzowski

D.G.   I think you know the role he played in Canadian literature. And you know that people are talking about what happened since and are saying: "There is no new Peter Gzowski. Maybe we've seen the golden days of discussing Canadian writing – discussing new, exciting Canadian writers." We've still got the writers but we don't have the media. We don't have a Peter Gzowski. We don't have a successful bookstore chain...

C.E.   *"Canada Reads" doesn't create as much interest as Peter Gzowski did?*

D.G.   Peter Gzowski did the equivalent of a "Canada Reads" every week. And that's the difference.

C.E.   *What are the most rewarding books you published?*

D.G.   You know, I run through the list and I don't know... The most rewarding ones are the ones I edited as well as published. But it's hard to single any one out. And some of them are out of print. And I feel special sorrow for those that, if you read them today, you would say: "This is pretty good, why don't I know more about this?" What grieves anyone who works in publishing is that luck plays a large role in whether the book will do well or not. And I, as the publisher, should be able to make sure that it works out.

(Pause)

Let me tell you about one that brings me special delight. One of my favourite books is *Dickens of the Mounted*. I went to a Vancouver-based humorist named Eric Nicol said: "Eric, Charles Dickens had a very unsuccessful son who had a disastrous twelve or fourteen years with the Canadian North-West mounted police, and what I would like you to do is to come up with fake diaries or letters home from this historical character and we will publish it as if it were real." And he loved this idea and so we really did publish them.

[Showing the book] This cover photograph really is of Francis Dickens. And this really is Fort Pitt, 1884, and he really did surrender that fort when there was the Riel rebellion. And then this really is the Canadian Encyclopedia entry on Francis Dickens who was a disaster, just a total failure[6]. Eric took that and researched it very carefully and we know from the historical records where Francis Dickens was stationed: he moved from this post, to this post, to this post. So we have a map showing quite accurately where he travelled and really was in all of those places. And then I did something really mischievous because I hired a calligrapher to write these letters. You'll notice the first one: "My dear friend, It was not the best of times, it was not the worst of times: it was Ottawa." And we said these had been discovered in the UBC library. And the result was, when this book came out, it hit the bestseller list both in non-fiction and in fiction because some newspapers were smart enough to say: "This is all a joke!" and others said: "No, this is true. Look at the photographs." So it was great.

There was an Encyclopedia of Canadian Literature edited by W.H. New four or five years ago, and their entry on literary hoaxes centered around this, and I'm happy to say, I was described as totally unrepentant.

---

[6] "Dickens, Francis Jeffrey, North-West Mounted Police inspector (born at London, Eng 15 Jan 1844; died at Moline, Ill 11 June 1886), third son of Charles Dickens. In 1864, after numerous unsuccessful career starts, Dickens joined the Bengal Mounted Police in India. He returned to England in 1871 and eventually obtained a commission in the NWMP in 1874. His unspectacular career was marked by recklessness, laziness and heavy drinking. He retired in 1886 and died shortly thereafter. Dickens can be blamed for worsening relations between the Blackfoot and the NWMP and for the growing antipathy of the officer cadre toward Englishmen." Canadian Encyclopedia.

C.E.   *When did you actually reveal the story?*

D.G.   Well it's revealed, for those who are very smart, right here on the back cover: "These witty and informative letters, revealed here for the first time, shed surprising new light not only on the Dickens family, but also on a wide range of characters, from Louis Riel and Sitting Bull all the way to Col. Harry Flashman." Now Flashman became a very popular fictional series, in Britain and beyond in the 1970s and 1980s. Someone named George MacDonald Fraser pretended to have discovered the Memoirs of Flashman. And our man Dickens comes across Flashman and describes him as a humbug.

So that was certainly one of the most rewarding books I published. Eric Nicol just loved the task and did very well with it.

Once you get me started on my favourite books, I could go on forever. But just one last story! I was recently involved in setting the historical record straight for a book called *Death on the Ice*. Harold Horwood passed away just a couple of weeks ago. And there was an obituary that said that he contributed the foreword to *Death on the Ice* by Cassie Brown. And it's such an important book, it came out in 1972 and it is still read by every Newfoundland school child. It's about a terrible incident when suddenly a hundred men were left on an ice-field in the Atlantic by mistake and seventy of them died and it's a wonderful account of the tragedy. The story of this book is one I'm especially proud of because Cassie Brown, who was a Newfoundland writer, came to me with a manuscript about this great disaster which was about thirty or forty thousand words long and I said: "This is an amazing story but you don't have enough material. Here is what you have to do: you have to research this, and that, and come back with all of that and the manuscript should be twice as long." And usually you do that – you give good advice – and you never see them again. It's too much work. But she came back and said: "Here is the book." And it was very good. It was extremely well-researched. But it was Harold Horwood – also a Newfoundlander – who was able to join in the project and bring in what I describe as the poetry. And that's why it's "Cassie Brown with Harold Horwood." Harold Horwood, in the foreword, said this is Cassie Brown's book, not mine. But I felt obliged since to say: "No, he did more than that. He contributed another six or seven thousand words. He added a paragraph here and a page there..." I sent that account to the Newfoundland papers because people there would be interested to know the exact details of his contribution. I thought: "I am the only person in the world who knows what happened: Cassie Brown is gone, Harold Horwood is gone." So I was able to set the record straight.

(Pause)

And then my favourite title is *How to Be Not Too Bad: A Canadian Guide to Superior Behaviour*, written by Charles Gordon. It's a response to American titles which are *How to Be Excellent, How to Be the Best*. But the Canadian guide is *How to Be Not Too Bad*. Not bad, eh?

PART II

DOUGLAS GIBSON'S VIEWS ON THE INDUSTRY

From Doubleday to Macmillan

C.E.   *The M&S Internet pages on your biography state that your entered the world of publishing in March 1968, as an editor with Doubleday Canada and that "through a series of accidents [you] found [yourself] running an editorial department at the age of 25." Can you tell us about this "series of accidents"?*

D.G.   The series of accidents was that I was hired when Doubleday Canada was starting up an editorial department and I saw, for the only time in my life, an ad for an "editorial Trainee" in the Toronto *Globe and Mail*. So I was hired as a trainee editor in March, and I went to New York in September, and I went through a training program in the Doubleday New York office – a week in the arts department, a week in the sales department etc. – and the man (David Manuel by name) who was setting up this department was supposed to continue there as a managing editor and I would come back and become an editor. But he was recalled to New York in December and he phoned me and said: "You'd better get back here fast and you'll sort of look after things until they find someone else." And they never got around to finding someone else. So I come back: I'm 25, and I don't know anything about editing. But they never got around to hiring a real, experienced editor. So I just edited books by doing what I thought needed to be done. And by the time they presumably got around to thinking: "We need an editor," they turned to me and said: "Well, you seem to know what needs to be done." So it really was a series of accidents. I was really lucky. And that's the way it continued until 1974 – which we will get to later.

C.E.   *What was the Canadian publishing world like when you first came to Canada?*

D.G.   Perhaps I'm the wrong person to ask about that because I was just so excited about being in the book world.

C.E.   *You could have been anywhere, as long as you were in that world!*

D.G.   Yes. I didn't know about the publishing world in Scotland, where I came from. I didn't know about it in the US – you know, I spent a year doing my Masters at Yale. And then my three months in New York gave me a pretty good sense of big, large-scale New York publishing. So the Canadian publishing world was a much smaller scene. And it was dominated by M&S and a few other small companies. M&S and Macmillan were the two major publishers. So I was busy learning about the publishing world and learning about Canada.

C.E.   *According to MacSkimming, in the 1950s, it was generally thought "that publishing was a profession for gentlemen, preferably gentlemen with English or Scots accents." (34)[1] Would you agree with this? Is that the impression you got when you started in publishing in the late 1960s?*

D.G.   I think that was a joke. There were, of course, lots of Scots around. But there were lots of Scots in the UK publishing world too. There was a great tradition of Scottish involvement in the book world, so that, for example, in the 19th century, people like John Murray, Constable, Nelson (they all were Scots[2]) went South, and set up publishing companies so that the Scottish tradition in publishing certainly continued in Canada with names such as M&S, Macmillan of Canada, Douglas & McIntyre… I'm amused by the mention, in the MacSkimming quote, of the English accent because the traditional Canadian reaction is to bristle a little when people with English accents tell them what should be done (but Scottish accents are OK). And Sir John A. Macdonald, the first Canadian PM said: "Oh, God save us from more over-washed Englishmen!" "Over-washed Englishmen!" is a wonderful phrase that all Canadians love. As for the "gentlemen" part, it is certainly true that publishing was regarded as a gentlemanly profession – and we will talk later about John Gray. I think John Gray exemplified that. It was, I think, like most professions in those days, also heavily male at the top. And this pretty much applied to every profession in the 1960s and 1970s in Canada – although there were extraordinary women like Gladys Neale, who ran the education department at Macmillan and who became a very powerful and leading woman in publishing. Since then as you know, there has been an upsurge of many talented women. But to come back to the quote, I think MacSkimming is joking there.

---

[1]   "[In the 1950s] trade publishing retained vestiges of colonialism, with all the self-doubt that condition entails. An editorial in the January issue of Quill & Quire admiringly cited a recent novel by David Walker… One of the characters in Walker's The Storm and the Silence was a publisher turned commando officer, who described his former profession as being "creative because you help other people to create." The anonymous editorialist opined that this character stood for good old-fashioned chivalry and asked rhetorically: "Is publishing, then – is the book business generally – one which attracts the chivalrous? Certainly it has little to attract anyone interested primarily in making money." (MacSkimming 34).

[2]   For more information on the Scotting printing and publishing tradition, see: http://www.scottishprintarchive.org.

C.E.   *You arrived on the publishing scene at the time of Canada's centennial. M&S had just launched seven series of books proclaiming their national identities[3]. Did you feel part of this national pride?*

D.G.   You're right that Canada's centennial was a remarkable time of awakening. As it happens, I recently gave a lecture on the 1960s in Canadian publishing and I called it "The long decade" because I said that Canada's 1960s ran from 1960 to about 1974-75, because that was the time when the Centennial celebration and Expo 67 led to an upsurge in interest in Canada and being Canadian – exemplified, as you said, by the M&S centennial history and so on. In turn, many new Canadian companies rose up. And, as a result of having more Canadian publishers, more and more Canadian writers were encouraged to write. And if you compare the number of titles published in, say, 1963, 64, 65, compared with this year, last year, it's just extraordinary. In fact, some years back then, in the Governor General's Award Competition, no novels were considered worthy of winning the prize and there were only ten novels published. So there is no doubt in my mind that 1967 had a huge impact in terms of morale. Suddenly, Canadians took a special pride in being Canadian, and started to explore what that meant in books and in publishing companies; a greater attention was paid to these books. And then, of course, there were Canadian bookstores that sprang up, devoting more time and attention to Canadian books.

C.E.   *But as far as you were concerned, you weren't excited about the centennial; you were excited about what the centennial brought about.*

D.G.   I was excited to be part of this and it's only in retrospect, through my studies and conversations, that I realized what a huge shift there was from the time before – which I did not know at first hand – to the excitement that I still find myself part of.

Media Coverage

C.E.   *What did you think of the media coverage for books in the 1960s? Apart from Robert Weaver's programs on the CBC (which started in 1954 with* Anthology?*), were there any other forms of support from the media to promote fiction? Did that change in the 1970s? Do you feel the media and literary criticism in Canada promotes the sort of books you would like to promote[4]?*

---

3   King 142.

4   In France the contributions of critics such as Barthes and Blanchot are greatly missed. Even "*Le Monde Littéraire*" has turned fairly commercial. Dominique Rabaté claims that new forms of literary criticism need to be developed (maybe via the Internet).

D.G.   Yes, the media coverage in the 1960s... I tended to pay attention more to the print coverage (the reviews, the attention given by the newspaper) than to what the CBC did. But you're right to single out Robert Weaver's program. I'm doing a biography of Alice Munro this fall by Robert Thacker, and he lays great stress on just how vitally important Weaver was in the career of Alice Munro and the lives of so many other writers.

C.E.   *Robert Weaver was the promoter of their work. He believed in their work...*

D.G.   Exactly, he encouraged writers such as Alice Munro to take themselves seriously as professional writers when no one else was. So his radio programme "Anthology" was terrific.

C.E.   *But you paid more attention to reviews?*

D.G.   Well, that was the way I was taught the game was played: you send out press releases, you send out various review copies and you desperately hope for good reviews in the papers.

C.E.   *In the main national papers and in the local papers?*

D.G.   Exactly. So I was less conscious then of the possibilities of other media being major publicity vehicles for books. And, to jump ahead, we reached a pinnacle of that in the 1990s, when Peter Gzowski's CBC program "Morningside," became a daily national conversation about books – extraordinary! And we know that booksellers would plead with us to tell them when an author was going to be on Peter Gzowski so they could stock up hundreds of books because they knew that the phone would start ringing as soon as Peter Gzowski would stop interviewing the author.

C.E.   *When I went to the Harbourfront Festival in 1998, Peter Gzowski interviewed Alistair MacLeod, and I really enjoyed hearing them both.*

D.G.   Well, Gzowski, in his shambling and apparently informal and unstructured way, was a wonderful interviewer and he knew exactly where he was going, although it seemed to be going nowhere. It was very good.

C.E.   *Coming back to the importance of press coverage...*

D.G.   Yes, I was saying that I was probably old-fashioned and believed that the newspaper coverage was what mattered. Later, I came to understand how important radio and television could be.

C.E.   *And when you send out press releases to the press, do you find that they simply recopy the information from your document and shape it into an article, or do the journalists actually read the book and come up with comments of their own.*

D.G.   Well before the 1970s, if the journalists did a general or in-depth review, then they would review it, but if they were lazy, then you would find that the flap copy from the book cover would form much of their review. But what changed in the 1970s was that, as more Canadian books came to be published, the Writers' Union got underway, and the Writers' Union started to do good work – missionary work – in contacting newspapers and saying: "Hey! This is ridiculous! You only do one book a week!" and they started visiting newspaper editors and publishers. They put proper pressure on the newspapers to do a better job. And then the cumulative effect of all this is that you have more Canadian authors producing fiction, and you have the Writers' Union making appropriate noise, and you have more bookstores springing up and selling more books. So, over time, you start to develop reviewers who are comfortable reviewing fiction because – and I jump back to my earlier point – when we first discovered that radio and television were becoming more important in selling books, the people in those media were much more hesitant about interviewing authors of fiction – they said, well fiction is so hard to talk about. But non-fiction is easy! "You wrote a book about… whatever…" But fiction! "Oh, how do you write? With a pencil?" And they found that that was hard, and that continues to be something that intelligent interviewers worry about.

So coming back to your initial question, yes, the change in the 1970s was that the media in general got better and started paying more attention to Canadian books, including fiction. And of course, the other thing that happened was that the 1960s were the launching decade (I called it the "long decade") for the major figures that I don't need to mention – Margaret Laurence, Mordicai Richler, Robertson Davies, Alice Munro, Margaret Atwood etc. As these writers were starting to gain attention outside the country, it washed back into Canada. People said: "My goodness! Oh, they must be good. They're getting major attention in London and in New York!" So that played into this upward spiral that I'm speaking of, and was very profitable for everyone.

Macmillan in the 1970s

C.E.   *In 1973, John Gray retired. M&S wanted to purchase Macmillan because of the profitability of its educational department but failed to do so. It was a tough time for the industry. That was just before you joined Macmillan. What was the atmosphere of the company like when you joined?*

65

D.G.   Well I was very amused to find how delightfully old-fashioned it was. The Macmillan people were in the old building that had actually been built for them in 1906. They had an old English lady who answered the switchboard and it was full of old-fashioned cord lines. At the end of the day (at five o'clock) she would simply pull all the cords. And that was it! In the morning and in the afternoon, a tea trolley went around. I think you could also get coffee, but tea was an appropriate drink. It was almost a Dickensian place. It was great fun! I was a young Turk and I was supposed to change things.

C.E.   *In 1974, you became Macmillan's trade editorial director. What prompted that move?*

D.G.   I'd been at Doubleday since 1968 and I had produced a lot of books (it was just me and an editorial assistant – a very small operation). I'd been there for 6 years, and I'd learned how to edit and publish. Macmillan, as I mentioned, was one of the two big names in town.

C.E.   *And you wanted to move to a bigger structure?*

D.G.   And they came to me. And what prompted that, I suppose, was that I spoke at Alberta, at an industry event and Hugh Kane was in the audience and I think he came back and said: "We should try to hire this bright young person!" And they asked me whether I would like to work at Macmillan's and I said: "What would I do?" and he said: "Well, we would like you to be in charge of our trade department and be Editorial Director." And that, of course, was a terrific thing because that was what brought me in touch with Hugh MacLennan and Marley Callaghan and Robertson Davies and W.O. Mitchell and so many great novelists of that generation. And then, of course, in turn, I brought in further people like Alice Munro, and Mavis Gallant and Jack Hodgins, in the years that I was there from 1974 to 1986.

C.E.   *You edited John Gray's autobiography,* Fun Tomorrow. *What struck you most about J. Gray's experience?*

D.G.   I liked John Gray immensely. Certainly, you've seen the photograph of him with the pipe in Roy Macskimming's book, and I don't know whether you can see, but he had a handkerchief up his sleeve, you know, like an English officer. And he was very much in that pipe-smoking generation. And he'd been in the war, and was such a modest gentleman that in *Fun Tomorrow*, he didn't get around to mentioning that he'd won a major military medal for his service. Something like a military cross.

C.E.   *Is his biography still in print?*

D.G.   Unfortunately, no. But it's a fascinating account of being a young man in the very old-fashioned world of Canadian publishing in the 1930s and then in the 1940s. And I think you know that it was extraordinary the way the book was completed and got into his hands before he died[5]. And I actually called John Gray's son and said: "Can you recall... Is this really the way it happened?" The account of this sounds too melodramatic, but this was indeed how it happened.

C.E.   *MacSkimming said you were the link between the "old" Macmillan and the new, and that you helped Besse handle the recent takeover (MacSkimming 319-321). How did you feel about the responsibilities that Besse was giving you (the head of the trade list, the departure of the trade personnel to new offices in the context of lay-offs and take-over by Gage, the pressure to make the trade division profitable)?*

D.G.   I was indeed the link between the "old" Macmillan and the new because I'd been there since 1974. But I didn't help Besse handle the take-over.

C.E.   *There's a very interesting portrait of Besse in MacSkimming's book (318-321).*

D.G.   Well, what happened there was that Besse really thought that he could take over the whole Macmillan line and do whatever he wanted with it, and that I and all the authors would automatically be happy. And the press – including the editorials in *The Toronto Star* and perhaps *The Globe and Mail* – were concerned about the potential loss of this fine cultural publisher. And so the press got behind me and said: "We hope that Douglas Gibson won't simply accept any terms." And there were lots of "viewing with alarm" letters and so on. And I was in a position to say: "Well, tell me what you have in mind because I'm not sure I want to stay unless I can do a proper job with our authors who are happy to stay." Of course, that's not what he wanted to hear, but acquiring Macmillan with me leaving and taking with me a large number of authors was not what he wanted, either, (and that's what would have happened, and that would not have been good for his business); so he said: "No, you continue to be the Publisher and drive things the way you did."

C.E.   *He took the counter-power you represented seriously enough to make a deal with you.*

D.G.   That's right. He said: "You continue to run the list, etc." And so, I was able to keep all of my people. And I take great pride in this because when a company is taken over, there is this great mood of

---

[5]   MacSkimming 67.

terror. I brought everyone in the editorial group together and I told them I'd keep them posted on what happened. So every week, we'd get together and I'd say: "All right, here's the latest news." And I kept all of these people, so we went as a unit. Everyone else was gone – you know, the sales people and other departments disappeared. But in this world, you do what you can, and what I did was keep the integrity of the editorial department, and as a result, the integrity of the publishing line and, in fact, the years from 1979 to when I left, were very good publishing years. We won lots of prizes. We introduced Guy Vanderhaeghe; we brought out Christina McCall's famous political book *Grits*[6]. She passed away just last week, so you may have seen a number of editorials about her.

I was the link between the "old" Macmillan and the new, and how did I feel about my responsibilities? I was glad to take them because I felt I could protect people, protect authors and protect an important cultural publishing programme. I had been running it very closely, and it worked.

But these things change, because Ron Besse had lost the battle but he continued the war. You know if you win over a dictator, the dictator remembers it. And so Besse brought in a business manager in 1983, and that wasn't a happy arrangement. And then he brought in Linda McKnight late in 1985. And at that point, I thought, well... And Avie Bennett approached me, having just bought M&S. So I thought "Macmillan is treating me badly – they're narrowing the list, and at the same time, they're bringing in other people." The story Avie tells is when he bought M&S, at the very end of 1985, he said to Jack McClelland: "So what should I do now?" And Jack apparently said: "Well, I'd try to hire young Gibson away from Macmillan." And Avie didn't know young Gibson, but he said OK and he arranged a meeting and that's how it happened.

C.E.   *So it was Jack McClelland's idea originally?*

D.G.   Yes.

---

[6]   Christina McCall was a writer of literary non-fiction who worked as a socio-political analyst for Maclean's, Saturday Night, and the Globe and Mail. Grits, her portrait of the Liberal Party, was acclaimed as "one of the most important Canadian books of the 1980s" and her work has won major awards.

Joining McClelland & Stewart
and Launching the Douglas Gibson Imprint

C.E.   *Your departure for M&S in 1986 coincided with a change of editorial direction at Macmillan's. Besse declared that "it was almost impossible to build a profitable business around fiction." (MacSkimming 321). Also, Macmillan's trade list considerably narrowed. How far do you think your departure had an effect both on Besse's belief in the business and on Macmillan's portfolio of authors?*

D.G.   I like the way you put that. Well yes. What happened in 1986 was, in effect, what would have happened in 1979, if he hadn't made a deal with me then. I left. And as you know, almost every one of the major authors left: "That's it. I don't like Besse. What's going on? Douglas Gibson has this imprint. That sounds pretty good." And I've heard people say in my presence: "What happened to Macmillan? They suddenly seem to have gone downhill."

C.E.   *Well, as long as the authors were protected and housed elsewhere...*

D.G.   Yes. I take no pleasure in having destroyed Macmillan's portfolio, but that's the way it happened. The authors chose to follow me and as you know, for many years, M&S benefited by having the best of Macmillan's list and the best of M&S's list. This was terrific.

C.E.   *Your recruitment at M&S gave you the opportunity to develop your own imprint. It was the first time a Canadian editor was given a personal imprint within a larger firm. Was this opportunity the main reason for your move to M&S?*

D.G.   The main reason for my move to M&S was that I wasn't happy at Macmillan's after 12 good years there, but the other reason was that Avie Bennett was coming to me here, saying: "Do you want to come and work here?"

C.E.   *He was giving you free rein...*

D.G.   Exactly! I thought: "My God, this is perfect!" I'd done the corporate stuff, and I'd spent my time worrying about who got this office, and what sort of raise the people on my team should be getting etc. And now suddenly, I'm doing the books, just the books! So it was a wonderful opportunity. And we invented the concept of an imprint to Canadian Publishing. How much freedom can you give? The publishing house can't just give me a blank cheque – "Oh, by the way, I've just spent half a million dollars!" So we built in some limits that seemed fair to both sides and, incredibly – that was 1986, we were inventing it – last year (2004) when I reverted back to that system, the old framework still worked.

C.E.   *So you picked up from where you left off?*

D.G.   Yes. Exactly. It seemed to have the proper amount of checks and balances and the proper amount of freedom for me.

C.E.   *Phyllis Bruce at HarperCollins also had his imprint. What is characteristic of the Phyllis Bruce imprint?*

D.G.   That came a little later. Phyllis is a very highly respected editor. I can't speak to the characteristics of her imprint but she does both fiction and non-fiction very well and she has very good authors. I don't know the details of her imprint arrangement, but I'm glad to see another imprint out there.

C.E.   *What are the other Canadian imprints you know about? Do you think this practice is likely to become more fashionable in the years to come?*

D.G.   I don't know of any others. Patrick Crean, who is with Thomas Allen now, had an imprint at Key Porter – I think that ran for a couple of years. But that's about it. And who knows whether it will become more fashionable? I know that for someone like me, it's a terrific arrangement because I'm skilled in not only the business of taking a manuscript and working on it and making it good and having the author approve, but in all the other aspects of publishing: "Here's the type of cover we should have for this... and the title should be... and we should have a sub-title...." all the publishing details that need to be focused on. I can and I'm very happy to do all of that. An editorial imprint might be a terrible mistake for someone who sees it as a refuge from the publishing part of looking after a title, because I see it very much as the two major responsibilities (editing and publishing) given to one person: you're the editor but you're the publisher and you're responsible for making all those clever and strategic decisions. And I love working on covers, and so on. If you're someone who's happy working in a miniature focussed publishing company of your own, then this is perfect. If you are a highly skilled editor who's not really so happy with all of the other aspects, or with promoting the book or selling the book to the sales force and so on, then it's perhaps not the ideal solution. Then I wouldn't recommend the arrangement I have. But for me, it's perfect. It's going to be interesting to see whether it does become more fashionable, because our society seems to be becoming more focussed and making use of freelance specialists – one person does this and then another does that. So it's an interesting question. I wish I knew the answer.

Changes at M&S

C.E.   *Avie Bennett changed things around considerably at M&S. Some of the recruitments he made were criticized – for example Adrienne Clarkson's (MacSkimming 322). Some were applauded – Bill Hushion in sales and marketing, Chris Keen with retail experience (323). What did you think of those changes?*

D.G.   Adrienne Clarkson is a very bright woman but she made a terrible mistake. I should really stress first that I had no contact with her. I was working with Avie Bennett. I very carefully was not interfering with Adrienne. And people would come to my office and say: "You'll never believe this!" and I would say: "I'm sorry, I don't want to hear this." Because the last thing she needed as a new publishing person was this highly experienced publisher sitting in another part of the building fomenting unrest. But what I couldn't help hearing sometimes or what I have heard since, is that she made the terrible mistake of pretending that she knew this stuff. All she had to say was: "I'm new to this. You're the experts, I respect your professionalism and experience. I will be drawing on that. So please, let's work together. And I will ask stupid questions. Please help me." And everyone would have helped. But instead, she pretended that she knew it. And it didn't work. Anyway, too bad.

C.E. *MacSkimming claims that "Hushion rebuilt the company's agency list by acquiring numerous British and American lines as ballast against the uncertainty of original publishing" (323). How did you respond to this measure?*

D.G.   Bill Hushion was an old, highly experienced sales and marketing person. Chris Keen was a very-well respected bookseller, the former head of Britnell's. So I think both of them were very clever hires. Bill Hushion had the old-fashioned belief – which may continue to be cor-rect – that a Canadian publishing company cannot function on its own without the support of ready-made agency books coming in from British and American publishers – as you know, you're not taking the risk of the publication, you're just saying: "Alright, you're publishing these in New York, we'll take a thousand and we'll sell them in Canada. And if that's not enough, then we'll ask you to send us another 500." It's a much safer way of surviving. And of course, selling those 1,000 or 1,500 copies supports your sales force and all of your infrastructure. So that was the traditional way for a Canadian publisher to survive if it was not supported by its educational lines – as Macmillan had been – or supported by the business of a home office publishing line – as the multinationals were. Logically, it made good sense and I was never opposed to taking on those agencies because the wisdom was that, of course, these agencies made money. Unfortunately, we carried out very careful studies and discovered that we were losing money on a number of the agencies. That was heresy; it came as a major surprise. So if you're doing something else to bolster your Canadian publishing and it's actually dragging it down, this is not good. So that was a surprise. But Bill Hushion was – and continues to be – an expert in this area (he now has his own company where he takes agency books from publishers).

C.E.   *M&S purchased Tundra Books in 1996. In 1972, you said publishing for children was a risky business[7]. Were you involved in the decision to purchase Tundra Books?*

D.G.   You found my 1972 quote about children publishing? It's good, isn't it?

It would not be fair to say that I was involved in the decision to purchase Tundra other than Avie saying: "I'm thinking of doing this. And what do you think?" and I probably said: "It makes financial sense. They've got a wonderful reputation." And with Kathy Lowinger, we knew we had someone who would maintain the tradition and keep the authors. So I was only peripherally involved but I was in approval and Tundra has been a good part of the M&S picture, and they continue to make money.

C.E.   *Avie Bennett sold off M&S's college list to Oxford in 1996. Did this decision affect you?*

D.G.   The decision affected us internally in that we had a managing editor whose special project – in addition to running the trade list – was to look after the college list. So when that went, half of his job went (he has now moved on to St John's).

C.E.   *So, it's a question of someone moving with the job and continuing elsewhere.*

D.G.   Yes. I think that the fact that we lost the sales force that was going in and out of university campuses meant that the sales of our literary series, the New Canadian Library suffered accordingly. You know the saying: "The best fertilizer is the farmer's foot on the ground." So if you don't have a sales force that is in and out of universities and colleges selling other things but also selling the NCL, your books are less in the minds of university professors when they're thinking about their recommendations to students. So I think that was a long term effect.

---

[7]   According to MacSkimming, you wrote in the Quill & Quire in 1972: "If all publishers are born gamblers, the men and women who publish children's books are the sort of people who jump out of tenth-story windows in the hope that an open truckload of mattresses will be going by." (275)

C.E.   *Your relationship with authors is long-standing. Many authors followed you from Macmillan's to M&S (Robertson Davies, Alice Munro, Mavis Gallant, W.O. Mitchell, Jack Hodgins and Guy Vanderhaeghe). How did these changes happen and how did the move from one publishing house to another affect your collaboration?*

D.G.   Robertson Davies had another book under contract (*The Lyre of Orpheus*) so he published that with Macmillan and then he came to me.

Alice Munro: Robert Thacker's book contains for the first time the letter that Alice Munro wrote to Macmillan saying why she wanted to leave them and follow me to the Douglas Gibson imprint. It's a wonderful letter where she explains that her wish to move is not anti-Macmillan, it's pro-Gibson. She doesn't dislike them; she really likes me and then she goes on to say why she really likes me and… it's wonderful.

C.E.   *When exactly is this biography coming out?*

D.G.   In September. And, incidentally, I wrote a funny piece in *Quill and Quire*, which will be coming out in their July issue, about what it's like for me to edit, not one, but two books, this fall – one biography of Alice Munro; one of W.O. Mitchell – where I'm a major character. And, as I said, it was a shock to find out that this fellow Gibson has led a far from blameless life.

As for your earlier question, W.O. Mitchell, Alice Munro, Mavis Gallant and Jack Hodgins each said: "Look, wherever you're going, I'm going with you." when I switched to M&S.

And then Guy Vanderhaeghe came later. And he has been very generous in saying: "Doug Gibson, my publisher from my first book to the last." So he and I are close, although I never edited him. The changes happened in slightly different ways with each author. And the move from one publishing house to another did not affect my collaboration at all in the case of the authors who joined the Douglas Gibson imprint because, as I explained to them: "It's going to be the same way. I was editing you at Macmillan, I will edit you here. And that's the new relationship." And they came because they liked that and because they knew what working with me as an editor and a publisher was like. The plan was that the move wouldn't affect the collaboration – I was offering a continuation of the same relationship.

C.E.   *Avie Bennett recruited you in the hope that some of the authors who had worked with you over the years would choose to join you. Was your recruitment mainly about quality or literary editing – operating this small "boutique" (where you took on only 5-10 books per year) and handling all publishing operations (from choosing the jacket and all other details, to supervising the book through the publishing process)?*

D.G.   I'd say it was about both literary and quality editing. I wanted to work only with the very best authors, ones I would enjoy working with, but also I wanted them to be successful. I was very selective. There were lots of people who said they wanted to work with me and in fact, a number of people I was able to steer to the general M&S list. And they were happy. Of course, after 1988, they knew that I would still be their publisher. There was a major difference from 1986 till 1988 when I took over as publisher. In 1986, I was able to say: "I'm doing 5-10 titles a year." After I assumed the overall role of publisher I could do only 2-3 Douglas Gibson Books titles per year and I turned all kinds of wonderful authors away. It would have been improper for me to be seen by my colleagues as stealing away all the best authors. So I would say: "Look, I can't do this." But what sometimes happened – and it happened for my own imprint with Peter Gzowski and James Houston who were regular M&S authors but they got to know me and said: "I'd like to become a Douglas Gibson book author." and I said: "Sorry, I can't do that." And Peter Gzowski said: "What if I stamped my foot?" And I said: "Well, you have to talk to Avie who will be a referee on this but you know that I'm saying I can't do this unless Avie says he wants to allow me in." So, in both cases, they went to Avie and Avie said: "That will be fine." And then for Alistair MacLeod (for both *No Great Mischief* and *Island*), I said: "Let me do this! I'm the right person for this!" But I didn't make these books Douglas Gibson books because Alistair was already a M&S author, and because there is a modest royalty arrangement involved in the Douglas Gibson books. So I would be a rich man… and it would have been inappropriate to take a book like *No Great Mischief* to my imprint.

C.E.   *A book with such financial potential…*

D.G.   Yes. And it was the same with the Trudeau autobiography, *Memoirs*. In all of the cases, I volunteered and said: "I want to work on this. I know it's not a Douglas Gibson book." As I said, I would be smoking cigars!

C.E.   *Were you involved in any other aspects of the publishing business?*

D.G.   As I told you, when I first joined, from 1986 to 1988, I carefully didn't get involved in any of the other stuff.

Becoming a Publisher

C.E.   *And in September 1988, you were promoted to the post of publisher. It then became your responsibility to oversee the company's entire trade list while continuing to edit your own authors.*

D.G.   The background there is that Avie came to me and said: "Look, it's not working with Adrienne. She'll be leaving. I'd like you to take over as a publisher." I said: "Hold on a minute, I've got this perfect job. No really, I mean, running the whole thing? The budgets – allocating the resources to this editor and that editor – I've already done that, at Macmillan. And my job right now is so much more fun! Why don't you find someone else?" And he said: "Why don't you think about it for a week?" And I said: "Why don't you think about finding someone else for a week?" And he came back a week later and said: "You know, I've worked with you, I'm sure you're the guy for the job here." And finally, he did a dirty thing, he said: "M&S is in trouble. It needs you." So I took on the role of publisher from 1988 onwards. And then I had the additional role of president in year 2000 – until about a year ago, May 2004.

C.E.   *Did Avie insist on having you by his side because he anticipated leaving the company some time in the future?*

D.G.   No. I don't think so. He enjoyed working with me and he thought that we would be a good combination – with him doing the overseeing of the financial aspects of the company and me looking after the books and the authors – and we worked very well together. A prominent lawyer named Michael Levine liked to call us "The Odd Couple, because, here is Avie who is a great character, who is keen on a drink, who comes from outside the book world, and then, here I am, a very focussed, abstemious, bookish character... and, of course, we were in and out of each other's offices for about 15 years and it was – and continues to be – a very fine relationship.

C.E.   *How much of your time did you manage to set aside in order to develop your own imprint? How much time did you spend editing and supervising other editors?*

D.G.   I'd say it was all week-ends and evening work. I was full-time supervising other editors, running the publishing department. Now, let me stress that supervising other editors tended to be a business of choosing to do this book rather than that book and then assigning an editor. I didn't look over the editors' shoulders at what they were doing, unless they said: "Look, I'm really having problems with this. What do you think?" You know, we had a very experienced and good editorial staff, so it was a question of assigning them. And sometimes, of course, I would need to say: "I think we're falling behind here. Are we going to get this in time?" You know, just the general management stuff. So that's what I did all day. I was responsible for developing the list of books we published, making sure that they came out, trying to make sure they were well-published and so on. And that involved working with marketing and sales and so forth. And my own editing – three to four books a year – was, as I said, all evening and week-end work.

C.E.   *Did marketing and sales change very much during that period?*

D.G.   Yes, it changed a great deal because Bill Hushion left and a guy named Ken Thompson came in from outside the book business.

C.E.   *Was that in the mid-1990s?*

D.G.   Yes, around that time. Avie brought him in to shape things up and to be a hard-driving sales manager from outside the book business. So he did that and he had a belief that I think was mistaken that everything depended on growth, so his obsession was to grow the agency line. This was the time when Chapters was growing and growing, so our sales went up and up, but then our returns went up and up and up. We were doing a lot more business each year but our profits were going down and down. So that was the major change. We tried huge expansion and a different way of selling and it didn't work as well as we hoped.

C.E.   *So did Ken Thompson stay on?*

D.G.   Well, when the company split up in year 2000; what happened was the publishing arm went with me, and he took what we called Stewart House which was the sales and agency distribution operation. He took them off and I'm afraid they went bankrupt. And that was terrible because, you know, there were people who could have gone either way and some people chose to go with him.

C.E.   *Ellen Seligman has also become a well-known editor at M&S, (working with authors such as Margaret Atwood, Michael Ondaatje, Jane Urquhart, Rohinton Mistry and Anne Michaels). Are you involved in helping her edit any of her authors' work? Do editors at M&S work mostly independently or do you feel the need to collaborate in any way? Why isn't there more than one imprint at M&S?*

D.G.   I've never been involved in helping Ellen edit any of her authors' work. Ellen is a very experienced and superbly skilled editor, so I simply stood back and gave her as much support as I could, but never looking over her shoulder. And yes, editors worked independently and I let them get on with it unless they came to me and said: "Do you think the tone of this preface is correct or not?" Or whatever. It might be a very small question but it was a case here of just seeking a colleague's second opinion.

C.E.   *Rather than sitting there on your own wondering what to do or not getting any further on a particular point.*

D.G.   That's right. And to turn to your question about why there isn't more than one imprint at M&S, I'd have to say that I can't really answer. No great decision was ever made: "We will only have one imprint." I couldn't say that. No. It just hasn't worked out.

C.E.   *You have partly answered my next question. I noticed on the Internet pages concerning your imprint, that you have kept the annual list very small. To avoid any conflict of interest with your role at M&S you encouraged many former authors to join the main M&S list, notably people like Ken Dryden, Guy Vanderhaeghe, Maggie Siggins, Robert Hunter, Michele Landsberg, Jeffrey Simpson and Roy MacGregor. Are these books you edited, or did you pass them on to another editor? On occasion you edited M&S books without adding them to your personal imprint (for example the* Memoirs *of Pierre Trudeau and Alistair MacLeod's books,* No Great Mischief *and* Island*). You put a lot of time and energy into editing those books, wouldn't it have made more sense to add them to your imprint? Do you feel any regret in having to limit the number of books with your imprint?*

D.G.   Yes, as we discussed, I did encourage former authors to join the M&S list. Maggie Siggins: that was interesting because I did work with her. But it wasn't a Douglas Gibson book. I did not edit Ken Dryden, although, to be fair, I did perhaps give an opinion. Guy Vanderhaeghe, no. Michele Landsberg, interestingly, has come back to me and is doing a Douglas Gibson book. Jeffrey Simpson's both was done with another editor – although my role was to think up that book, *The Friendly Dictatorship*, and he wrote a very nice word of introduction saying Doug Gibson gently prodded me into doing this book etc. And Roy MacGregor, no I found an editor for him. So in every case, I passed them on. And then we talked about why I didn't edit Trudeau and Alistair MacLeod. And yes, I feel regret in limiting the number of books in my imprint but, on the other hand, we all do the best we can in the time available to us.

C.E. *Your imprint continues to represent your personal interests (as stated on the web pages, these interests are eclectic – fine fiction, history, public affairs, humour, the great outdoors, the sea, the Rockies and the adventures of risk-taking travellers). How do you determine the sort of balance you're looking for, for your imprint? Do you often turn books down?*

D.G.   It will take me a while to answer that one…

C.E.   *How about my next question: Your list of authors has always been very impressive. Can you tell us about your experience with each one of them?*

Robertson Davies, Alice Munro, Mavis Gallant, W.O. Mitchell, Jack Hodgins and Guy Vanderhaeghe...

D.G.   I could spend the rest of the day over these two questions. Could we jump over that one too and come back to it later?

C.E.   *Yes, of course.*

Fiction / Non-Fiction

C.E.   *Your non-fiction list includes John Sawatsky, Andy Russell, Barry Broadfoot, Myrna Kostash, Harold Horwood, Don Starkell (author of* the classic Paddle to the Amazon*), James Houston (*Memoirs of an Igloo Dweller*, and other titles) and Peter Gzowski (*The Private Voice*, and other titles). How is your work on non-fiction editing different from your work on fiction?*

What can you tell us about your collaboration with non-fiction authors?

D.G.   I once went to Vancouver and delivered a 3-hour seminar on the differences between editing fiction and non-fiction. The young people there all came into the classroom believing that of course editing fiction was different to editing non-fiction, where I had approached the writing of the lecture from the basis that editing fiction and non-fiction was basically the same and – I'm sure you'll recognize this process – in preparing the lesson, my thinking changed. So, in fact, I announced to them, as a great revelation: "The two are different!" And they, of course, said yeah, yeah. And I said, no, no, no, you have to understand, I, throughout my career, have believed that it's essentially the same and it's only now that I've come to the conclusion that it is different. The difference is that in non-fiction, a good editor has to approach the book, to some extent, in the manner of a prosecuting attorney who asks questions: "Can you prove this?" "But how can you say this?" He has to attack the thesis and make sure that it stands up... So he approaches it in an almost hostile fashion to be sure that what remains after all the punching is solid. And fiction, I think, you have to approach in a generous spirit. You have to accept that the author has created this world, so, of course, you're still going to say but this, this and this doesn't make sense. But the approach, I think, shouldn't be so prosecutorial.

So, this was my great revelation, and the audience sat there yawning.

It is interesting though because, physically, I follow the same procedure: I read with a pen in my hand. Well first, I read (whether it's fiction or non-fiction) and then I think. And that's perhaps the most important part of the process. And then I go through, pen in hand, and I make notes and so on... But as a result of the thinking, I may be aware that we need to shorten this, and then we need more here because this isn't explained. And then I maintain a correspondence on the margins of the manuscript – I'm a very old-fashioned pencil person. So that's my collaboration with fiction and non-fiction authors – it's the same thing. I go through the same process but with a slightly different attitude – as I've explained. So I hope that makes sense.

C.E. *What is the next non-fiction book you've been working on and you're most excited about?*

D.G. I'm just about – in the next coming weeks – to bring out a book by a man called *Stephen Harper and the Future of Canada.* This is going to be a very controversial book because Stephen Harper, as you know, is likely to be the next Prime Minister. But he will be a surprise candidate. I'm proud to say that when I signed up this particular book, he seemed a very distant prospect and now he's likely to be our next Prime Minister. So there we are – Douglas Gibson once again getting into the midst of exciting action. And, last fall, my non-fiction list included an autobiography by Peter C. Newman and it was a number 1 bestseller and the book title was: *Here Be Dragons.* It was very controversial but it did very well.

C.E. *How about the fiction books?*

D.G. I think you know that Alice Munro's *Runaway* was a huge success. So last fall, for my first season "back to the fun part," I had a Christmas book by Alistair MacLeod (*To Every Thing There Is a Season*), *Runaway*, by Alice Munro. Peter C. Newman. Sheila Copps, an outspoken Canadian politician – her book was very controversial but was actually less accurate than we would have wished. That was something that came out after the publication of *Worth Fighting For.*

C.E. *The things that she wrote were challenged?*

D.G. I am afraid so.

And then, I had a new collection of stories by Jack Hodgins (*Damage Done by the Storm*). So that was my first list. It was spectacularly successful.

So, the non-fiction list continues, although, looking sadly at the non-fiction authors, Barry Broadfoot passed away two years ago, James Houston passed away a month ago (and I'm going to Connecticut to speak at his funeral a few days after I return from my mission in Scotland). And Peter Gzowski passed away two years ago.

My collaboration with non-fiction authors is that, usually, we become friends. And you'll see in the newspapers the obituary of Robert Hunter, the founder of Greenpeace; he was one of my authors and he became a good friend, and I'm going to his funeral. It's been a terrible time.

The Next Generation of Authors and the Role of Agents

C.E.   *How do you feel about the next generation of literary authors? Have you identified promising talents in M&S's portfolio?*

D.G.   There are good people coming up all the time. I was involved in signing up promising talents in M&S's portfolio. I can't take the credit, as publisher, of spotting them in most cases, but I can take the credit for having said: "Oh yes, this person is very good, we should publish her." And sometimes it's fiction under Ellen Seligman's banner – she has lots of promising young people. And sometimes, it's non-fiction; and we have a number of terrific young people coming up there.

C.E.   *What is the procedure? Do the M&S editors first spot young talents and then come to you for advice?*

D.G.   It used to be that they were thrown on the table at an editorial meeting and there would be a salesperson there who would say: "Can I read the outline?" I would be chairing all of this and in the end say: "OK, it seems everyone is keen on Laura Penny and why don't we offer so and so etc." The editor would then make the approach to the author and the agent. And that is one thing you haven't mentioned in your questions yet, and that is the rise of the literary agent in Canada. When I started out, there was one literary agent at The Canadian Speakers' and Writers' Service in Canada, and some Canadian authors had New-York based agents but most people we dealt with didn't have agents. And then, through the 1970s, and more specifically through the 1980s, a number of literary agencies sprang up, and in the 1990s, they were concentrated under the Westwood agency which now has, I'd say, 75% of the major Canadian agents. So that's been a major change. And literary agents tend to be very interested in the advance money that the publisher will offer for a book. And, guess what? The larger multinational companies are better able to risk paying large advances than the smaller Canadian companies. So I see the two things going hand in hand: the rise in the 1990s of the multinational companies – Knopf Canada, Random House Canada, Doubleday, Harper Collins, Penguin and so on – rising up because they've got big wallets and the agents tend to be impressed by that and go to the big companies, and they, in turn, get the good books and do very well. So that's been the pattern in the last 15 years. And I see the two going hand in hand. It's very hard for the smaller Canadian companies in general not being bankrolled by the multinationals. So. There you are. Something to consider.

C.E.   *M&S has an incredible ability to inspire loyalty in many of the country's leading authors. Do you think the company will also attract the next wave of literary authors?*

D.G.   Yes. M&S does have an incredible ability to inspire loyalty. But will it also attract the next wave of literary authors? Well there is the problem with the agents. M&S did very well in the Jack McClelland days because Jack McClelland personalized the company and he established personal relations with so many of the authors and their loyalty was to Jack and M&S. And Avie Bennett did a good job in retaining most of them – though not all – and I think we (and I include myself) have done a good job in maintaining the M&S tradition and people are proud to belong to that. We're about to take a major step in that direction next year because next June will mark the start of the celebration of the one-hundredth anniversary of M&S and we will be doing a lot of things between June and December. I'm the *éminence grise* for putting together a publication to mark this anniversary. And I think I can say now that I have arranged for a M&S historical display in the exhibition in the National Library in Ottawa and that will be terrific. Carl Spadoni is going to be the curator for it. And I'm very excited about that. And then we're going to be doing many other one-hundredth anniversary things (any Canadian company that is 100 years old, is quite a large deal). And this 100-year old Canadian company that has survived in the perilous trade for all those years is quite remarkable. So yes, it's going to be a big deal. And I hope it's going to be help in securing the loyalty of the older authors and attracting the next generation of authors, because these events are intended to remind the old loyal authors of their pride in the links with M&S.

C.E.   *Do you think one of the reasons the literary agents and the multinationals are so successful with the next wave of authors is that they can negotiate things which are outside of the realm of publishing – like movie rights or other business deals?*

D.G.   Well, I think they certainly talk a lot about that possibility. In my experience, the movie possibilities are often discussed but they don't actually happen. It's notable that younger authors nowadays – in their early twenties – rush to get literary agents and there are a lot of agents out there who are competing for young authors. Whereas by contrast, Alice Munro – and she talks about this in her biography – went for many years with no agent, and she remarks in amazement how impatient young authors are to get into print and have their agents and make great deals. So the attraction of the agents for young authors and the attraction of multinationals with their large wallets is a syndrome which I think you might look out for. It's certainly been increasing in the last 15 years.

Avie Bennett's Decision to Donate, and Sell and Doug Pepper's Arrival

C.E.   *In June 2000 you became President and Publisher of McClelland & Stewart. What did this new experience entail?*

D.G.   It entailed my learning that while I had been a publisher for 12 years and I had been a publisher for Macmillan for many years before that, that was all good and fun, but being the president of the company was all the part that is not fun. So it was all worrying about...

C.E.   *Sales, distribution...*

D.G.   And my time coincided with disasters in the retail sector and so I found that although I learned a lot when I became president – I learned about the importance of board meetings and the importance of keeping your board well-informed, and so on – at this time when I came in as a president, it wasn't an easy role to play. And I can't say that I found the president part nearly as much fun as the publishing part. The new experience entailed running a company in difficult times.

C.E.   *Avie Bennett donated the other 75% of his shares to the University of Toronto which, in the end, was perceived as a generous gesture benefiting future generations of Canadian authors. But at the time of the deal, the public worried about the 25% of the shares that were sold to Random House. Many authors (Margaret Atwood included) gave Bennett their support. How did that affect the public? How did your support affect the public?*

D.G.   There's no doubt that Michael Ondaatje and Margaret Atwood publicly supporting the donation to the University of Toronto affected the public. And I think I represented continuity and people thought: "Oh, Douglas Gibson who has been the publisher since 1988, he's staying on? Well! Yes, it's going to be the old M&S."

C.E.   *How did the change of ownership affect the members of the staff at McClelland & Stewart?*

D.G.   Well there was the split in the company between Stewart House which went on its own, and our own people who kept their jobs. So from having two floors in the office, we were down to one floor and there was a lot of anxiety that always goes with corporate change. But I think the major public concern was also the major internal concern about what the 25% ownership of Random House really entailed in terms of doing things differently. There has been a lot of shifting the schedule of books to accord with the selling season of the Random House sales force (which is the sales force we now use), so there's been a movement in that direction and, you know, that's a change, and any change leaves people uneasy.

C.E.   *Is the University of Toronto control sufficient to guarantee McClelland & Stewart's allegiance to Canadian authors and "editorial freedom"?*

D.G.   Well, it really comes down to profitability because the company has not been profitable. And the University of Toronto would be delighted to have an asset that makes money. So the future of the company and the University of Toronto control depends on the company doing well financially. So that's up in the air.

C.E.   *But how do you work with them? Are there any professors involved in the publishing?*

D.G.   No. The University has a majority of very active board members but on the ground...

C.E.   *They don't make any contribution to editorial work?*

D.G.   No. Because they have their academic press that is for scholarly work. And so there is no collaboration. The university organizes its publishing activity through the University of Toronto Press and the only collaboration is at the fringes. For example we would have our launch party in a building at the University of Toronto, or we would hold meetings at the University of Toronto.

C.E.   *So you use the premises occasionally but you get no editorial help from University of Toronto.*

D.G.   We don't. They're very interested in McClelland & Stewart continuing to be a fine publishing operation with which they want to be associated. So they're protective in that sense. But active? No.

C.E.   *McClelland & Stewart now focuses on the editorial, design and production functions, plus rights and promotion. Everything else is handled by Random House of Canada. How do you feel about the return of McClelland & Stewart editors to core creative roles? Do you think it best serves Canadian authors?*

D.G.   M&S editors continue to be at the centre of their creative publishing roles. Their roles haven't really changed. Since I moved sideways, the editorial department has been cut back a little but so has the number of titles. Obviously, I'm sorry to see good editorial people go. But the others who are here I think enjoy the same editorial freedom as before.

C.E.   *The more established the editor and authors are, the more editorial freedom they have. And what about your relationship with the*

Random House management? What are the main changes that you have noticed at McClelland & Stewart since the arrival of Doug Pepper?

D.G.   Just as I took care not to focus on any discontents, when Adrienne Clarkson was there, I'm very careful now with the present situation.

C.E.   *And I imagine it does pay off because you're giving this association a chance!*

D.G.   Absolutely. And the reason Doug Pepper hasn't heard a word of criticism coming from me is because I haven't said a word of criticism. And Doug is doing a tough job – I did it, so I know.

C.E.   *The best way you can help him is by focusing on your things.*

D.G.   And by making my books very profitable. And, as you know, last fall, four of my titles hit the bestseller list. So this is what I can do. And I work very hard at it.

"Back to the Fun Part"

C.E.   *In an article in* Maclean's *entitled "Back to the Fun Part," you said that you were looking forward to spending more time on editing. Apparently you have managed to devote a lot of time to editing lately – from editing Munro's last volume of short stories to working with Mavis Gallant this winter. Can you tell us a little bit more about your recent achievements?*

D.G.   I'm glad you got the article in *Maclean's*, "Back to the Fun Part." I thought, from the title onwards, that was exactly right. Also, I spoke quite openly about how the bookstore chains just threw out the window their precise agreements, and that was what put us in terrible trouble instantly. They'd promised not to return more than 30%, and our returns that year were 46%. And we had worked out our budget: Ok, we've sold this, and what we'll be getting back is 30% and suddenly, it was 46%! And we're facing this huge loss for the year. Every other Canadian publisher suffered in the same way but none of them had made this sort of public statement. And the Maclean's people were alarmed to see this potentially libellous statement and they went to their lawyer: "Can he say this?" And the lawyer was Julian Porter – husband of Anna Porter – and apparently he said through gritted teeth: "Everything Doug says is absolutely true." That's a very hard-hitting statement.

C.E.   *The returns go against the Code of Conduct. Will the government be taking action?*

D.G.   We'll get to that later. That's one of the questions in your questionnaire.

So. "Back to the Fun Part." This spring I published a book called *Rollercoaster* by James K. Bartleman about being Jean Chretien's foreign policy advisor from 1994 to 98. And it's a terrific account of what politics at the highest level is really like. Stephen Harper's biography – which is going to be hot stuff – we're rushing to get out. And then this fall, the books I mentioned earlier: *The Quotable Robertson Davies* by James Channing Shaw – a collection of approximately eight hundred quotations selected from Davies's written works; the biography of Alice Munro; the biography of W.O. Mitchell; and a wonderful new novel by William Weintraub – he's a contemporary of Mordecai Richler and Mavis Gallant. He's 75 years old and he's written a number of novels in the past. He wrote a marvellous non-fiction book called *City Unique* – about Montreal in the 1940-60 period, when it was a very sinful city, full of brothels and so on. But his new book is a coming of age novel, set in 1948. It's about an 18-year-old McGill student who desperately wanted to lose his virginity. His uncle Morty takes him to a strip club and he falls in love with the stripper. And it's a very funny book about the stripper in this idealistic young man's life. That's the book I'm doing this fall.

C.E.   *What are Weinstraub's other novels?*

D.G.   He wrote a novel called *Why Rock the Boat?* and another called *The Underdogs* – but that was 20 years ago. He has been compared to Evelyn Waugh and he's very good. So I say: look out for falling prizes!

C.E.   *This book has potential!*

D.G.   Yes! So, anyway. I do 5-10 books a year. Oh, and recent achievements? I go back to being a full-time editor and – lo and behold! – to my surprised pleasure, I'm one of the three nominees for our Editor of the Year – which is going to be announced in June.

C.E.   *This prize is given by the bookseller community, isn't it?*

D.G.   Yes. It's given at the Book Expo. It used to be called the Canadian Bookseller Association Convention and it's now called Book Expo. There are awards given for the Publisher of the year (and M&S is one of three nominees for this year) and Editor of the year and Author of the year where Alice Munro is a nominee. So we'll see.

We'll run through the next series of questions fairly quickly because we're running out of time.

The Government's Policies and Decisions in the Last Decades

C.E.   *In 1970, there was a famous demonstration against American take-overs (Graeme Gibson climbed onto the Ryerson stature in front of Ryerson Polytechnical Institute[8]) and this event received a lot of media coverage. Did you take part in any of the demonstrations?*

D.G.   I didn't take part in any of the demonstrations but I was in the crowd.

C.E.   *How did these demonstrations affect you?*

D.G.   I felt guilty that I was working for a multinational at that time, but on the other hand, I was seeking out Canadian authors and pushing Canadian books. And when I went on to moving to a Canadian company, I did the same sort of thing.

C.E.   *The advent of superstores, mainly Coles's first superstore in 1980, Chapters in 1995 and later Indigo in 1997, moved Canadian books into the mainstream. Before the late 1990s, author Peter Newman recalls that Canadian books were kept "on back shelves in small sections [of small, independent stores], titled Canadiana. They were just another category like gardening or the occult."[9] Has this Canadiana image completely disappeared? Do you agree that the emergence of superstores has helped to promote Canadian-authored books?*

D.G.   I'm not sure that I agree that the emergence of superstores has helped to promote Canadian-authored books. There may have been a time when they did, but right now the one Canadian superstore has a King Kong-like effect on the market. If they like a book, then that's great. But if they dislike a book, then it's automatically in great trouble.

C.E.   *According to one testimony on the DCH report, the superstores are indeed very damaging now, but in the 1980s, they weren't: they actually gave Canadian-authored books more visibility.*

D.G.   That's true. The situation changed in the 1990 and I spent a lot of my time as president worrying about getting paid by these chains.

---

[8]   "[In 1970] Canadians woke up to this takeover with the sale of a venerable Canadian educational publisher, W. J. Gage and the similarly venerable, United Church-owned, trade oriented Ryerson Press to Scott Foresman and McGraw-Hill respectively. There was also a major incursion into the Quebec market by the French publishing giant, Hachette." John Hutcheson, "Culture and Free Trade," in Coming of Age: Readings in Canadian History since World War II, Harcourt Brace & Company Canada, Ltd, Toronto, 1996, p. 460.

[9]   Newman, Peter C., "Letter to the Chair of the SCCH," 27 March 2000 (see SCCH report, reference n° 11).

C.E.   *In 1995, the Competition Bureau allowed the merger between Smith Books and Coles to go ahead. Did that come as a surprise to publishing houses? Did this merger accomplish anything for the industry?*

D.G.   We tend to assume now that the Competition Bureau is going to allow anything.

C.E.   *In 1999, the Competition Bureau agreed to the creation of Pegasus Wholesale. How did publishers view Chapters and Pegasus then?*

D.G.   Pegasus Wholesale was clearly a racket. It was the old Chapters warehouse to which we had been shipping the books and then suddenly: "Oh no! It's Pegasus! So we want an extra discount!" It was always a scheme to extract more money from publishers for doing exactly the same thing.

C.E.   *The Bureau also approved the merger between Chapters and Indigo. Although no buyer was found for the superstores which were on sale, the Bureau did not review the situation of Canada's biggest bookseller. Do you think this merger should have gone ahead?*

D.G.   I think they should have built tighter guidelines. And we saw the lack of them in the incidents I was describing.

C.E.   *Stoddart's General Distribution Services entered bankruptcy in spring 2002. How did the Canadian public react?*

D.G.   It was just terrible and the Canadian public reacted with a sense of: "Oh, no! More doom and gloom from Canadian publishing!" I've done some missionary work in explaining why this is.

C.E.   *At that time, there was an article which dismissed Canadian publisher's troubles on the grounds that the multinationals were publishing most of the important fiction. The article included examples of the publications from the Canadian houses of Random House, Knopf, Harper Collins, and Penguin. Do you feel there is a major difference in policies between Canadian publishers and Canadian outposts of foreign publishers?*

D.G.   I have a historical sense that the Canadian outposts of foreign publishers are particularly vulnerable to changes at head office. I've seen many Canadian outposts start up a trade publishing Canadian program with great beating of drums – and sometimes it would be Prentice Hall or sometimes it would be Fleet Publishers and sometimes it would be McGraw-Hill, sometimes it would be Little Brown. And then there is a change at head office and they close down the Canadian operation. And so if you are an outpost, you're vulnerable to politics at the imperial centre and that's a major concern. As for the differences in policies, I think I have referred to that. The Canadian outposts, if they are bolstered by, say, all the Harper Collins lists from the States, then they have already paid for their sales force and all of the people in the office, so that is subsidizing the Canadian books they publish – and that's fine; we should be drawing on that. But it makes it hard for anyone not so subsidized to compete.

C.E.   Quill & Quire *deplored that Canadian ownership, whether in publishing or in bookselling, counted for so little*[10]. *How do you explain such conflicting views about the evolution of the Canadian book industry?*

D.G.   It's woven right through Roy MacSkimming's book and I share the opinion that the government will never intervene to stop any sale going through. The record is now clear enough.

C.E.   *But if the industry started putting more pressure on the government or doing more effective lobbying, would it work? Is it a desirable thing? Or is it just not built into the country's logic?*

D.G.   I think it's not built into the country's logic. It depends, to a large extent on the personality of the minister involved. And the bureaucracy. But I can't see that some surge of public feeling would put real pressure on the government.

C.E.   *In November 2002, the government permitted Susan Stoddart, CEO of Distican to sell her company to its major American agency, Simon & Schuster*[11]. *The official explanation for the Distican ruling was that it the only way to save eighty Canadian jobs. Do you share this view?*

D.G.   I don't know the details of case.

---

[10]   According to MacSkimming: "Quill & Quire took the position editorially that Canadian ownership, whether in publishing or in bookselling, counted for little compared with the virtues of 'competition'.

The fact is that, in the long run, competition will decline and largely disappear if Canada's unique policy model is abandoned to raw economics. Diversity and competition in the Canadian book industry will be replaced by the dominance of a very few multinationals with no allegiance to this country. And precedents will have been established that allow any Canadian publisher, or for that matter Chapters/Indigo, to argue that the government has given itself no choice but to let them sell to foreign buyers." (389).

[11]   According to MacSkimming "S&S had reportedly stated it would refuse to work with any new Canadian owner of Distican, as the policy required; instead it would pull out of Canada, which represents about 7% of its $649-million (US) operations, and go home. Executives at S&S's parent, Viacom, knew from experience how effective it can be to threaten the Canadian government" (388).

C.E.   *What do you think of Amazon.ca situation?*

D.G.   Strangely, I'm in favour of it. This is what would happen in the past (and we've checked this when Alice Munro brought out a US edition); when Canadian subscribers ordered a copy of a Canadian book, they got the American edition. We had employees here in Toronto ordering that Alice Munro book and they got American edition and so we were losing millions of dollars because Amazon always took the American edition. But since they set up dot ca, we've been getting the Canadian edition.

C.E.   *And this is something you have control over? Is there a risk of them changing this?*

D.G.   Certainly when they set up in Canada, they said they were going to do that and they have done it: it's been very beneficial to us. So I'm all in favour of that.

The Situation of the Book Industry Today

C.E.   Many industry practices have been under fire lately. You have been known to denounce a number of them.

Can you comment on the following examples:

– the excesses of what you termed "cheque-book publishing" (369).

– the retailers' abuse of book returns and many other commercial practices at the distribution level (in the Maclean*'s interview, you said the Indigo return rate was as high as 50%).*

D.G.   "Cheque-book publishing" is where you pay huge sums of money to acquire a major author and then you throw huge sums of money into the promotion of the book to justify having put huge sums of money into the book.

C.E.   *That is linked to the role of the agent.*

D.G.   Yes. And the problem with that is that you're chasing best-sellers. Nine times out of ten, you're doing that with someone who is already a best-selling author, and you want another of the same. It's not linked to creative publishing.

The Indigo return rate: I know one publishing company was up at 75% returns and almost put out of business because of it. It's a nuisance and I believe things are getting better, but not spectacularly. But what we discovered with the Competition Bureau legislation is that they weren't going to take any action unless an individual publisher made a specific complaint to Indigo. And Indigo made it clear that they would viciously punish anyone who went after them for excessive returns. So the legislation proved to be useless.

C.E.   *How do you view the government's apparent retreat from its policy objectives? Do you feel the legislation needs to be reviewed*[12]*?*

D.G.   Again, it's not in the country's logic to intervene, and as I said, I'm not sure they could do so effectively.

C.E.   *What did you think of the outcome of the round tables organized by the Canadian Heritage in 2000*[13]*?*

D.G.   I don't know about the outcome of the roundtables. I don't think an awful lot happened.

C.E.   *Do you agree with MacSkimming who claims that: "In some respects, book publishing is regressing to conditions of the 1950s and 1960s"?*[14]

D.G.   I think that's an interesting comment.

I'm now speeding down your list of questions because we're running out of time.

C.E.   *What do you think of the competitive situation today? Will diversity and competition decline in favour of the dominance of very few multinationals?*

D.G.   Yes, I worry about that.

C.E.   *How did your dealings with the distribution network change with the advent of superstores? Does the distribution organization affect the way you edit books today? Does it affect the way other publishing houses work?*

D.G.   There's a real danger there, that stupid publishing houses, when they're considering buying a book, will go to the distributor and ask: "What do you think of this book? Would you buy it?" And then, in effect, key responsibility would lie with the chain which occupies 70%

---

[12] The "Competition Act" (which examines unfair competition practices such as the ones brought about by vertical or horizontal integration), the "Investment Canada Act" (which reviews all investments by foreign investors), the 1997 amendments to the Copyright Act (which includes ruling against the "parallel importation provisions") and the "Excise Tax Act."

[13] The report of the Committee (the SCCH report) can be found at the following address: http://www.parl.gc.ca/InfoComDoc/36/2/HERI/Studies/Reports/heri01/04-toc-e.html.

[14] "One of those conditions, clearly, is the imbalance between the Canadian-controlled and foreign-controlled sectors. Others include the dilemma in retail book-selling, the state of school libraries, and inadequate media coverage" (MacSkimming 389).

of the market. And that is something I think is a terrible danger because it can happen innocently: "Well, let me just check this with the sales manager…" and then you get a bad response and you come back and say: "Let's not publish the book." Or if you get a good response, you'll say: "Yes, let's do it." And that's a real major concern. And I'm sure there must be publishing houses – I wouldn't quote any because I don't know – who are now reacting according to what they hear back when they're considering a book. So you can see instantly what a danger this is, with the book chain in effect making publishing decisions for publishers.

C.E. *What do you think of the book distribution network in Canada today? Would you say there is a shortage of community-based, independent retailers or do you feel book distribution needs to enter a new era?*

D.G.   Yes, there is a shortage of independent retailers. I just heard the Double Hook bookstore in Montreal is going out of business. That's very sad. I'm sure that the book distribution will enter a new era. Eventually, we'll get into the business of printing on site in individual bookstores and that will help Canadian publishing more than any other country's publishing because we're dealing with such huge distances and spending so much money trucking heavy cartons of books to and fro.

C.E.   *What do you think of Amazon.ca, Indigo.ca and other e-tailers?*

D.G.   I wish them well because in e-tailing, you're not looking at returns. You're looking at getting books to people who really want them. It's a wonderful advance.

C.E.   *Which also allows for a huge database of book references.*

D.G.   Yes. And that's good for readers.

C.E.   *Is McClelland & Stewart thinking of going into POD? Are you interested in developing any of the niche markets in publishing?*

D.G.   POD: we've done a little bit of that and, I don't know about M&S, but I sense that we're going to be doing more niche marketing because the computer allows us to get at more specific markets than in the past.

C.E.   We'll skip the next two questions which you have already answered: What do you consider to be the government's role in relation to the publishing industry?

How would you like to see your relationships with other industry players evolve? (your relationships with other publishers, with prospective authors, with the distribution network, with leagues and syndicates, with the professional press, with the media).

What are your recommendations to the different industry players today?

D.G.   Don't trust the chains.

Focus on books. The books are what last in this thing – not the distribution system.

Correspondence

Letter from Alice Munro to Douglas Gibson
November 30, 1985

Reprinted from: Thacker, R. 2005. Alice Munro: Writing Her Lives:
A Biography. *Toronto: McClelland & Stewart, 419-420*

Doug first talked to me about publishing with Macmillan in the mid-1970s. I was very discouraged at that time. Ryerson had done nothing to promote or even to distribute my first book. MacGraw-Hill Ryerson had published the second with expressed reluctance and the third without enthusiasm – merely, I believe, to keep a Canadian fiction writer on their list. Every publisher I had met had assured me that I would have to grow up and write novels before I could be taken seriously as a writer. No one in Canada had shown the least interest in taking on a writer who was going to turn out book after book of short stories. The result of this is that I wasted much time and effort trying to turn myself into a novelist, and had become so depressed that I was unable to write at all. Doug changed that. He was absolutely the first person in Canadian publishing who made me feel that there was no need to apologize for being a short story writer, and that a book of short stories could be published and promoted as major fiction. This was a fairly revolutionary notion, at the time. It was this support that enabled me to go on working, when I had been totally uncertain about my future.

I came to Macmillan because of Doug, and his respect for my work changed me from a minor, "literary" writer who sold poorly into a major writer who sold well. I hope that you will understand how I have felt, from that time on, that I owe him a great deal, and that I want him to have charge of any book I publish. I am not making a judgement against Macmillan – my relations in the house have always been good – but for Doug Gibson.

I realize that I do not have a legal right to move this book, but I hope that my very strong feelings about publishing with Doug will influence you to let me go.

Letter from Robertson Davies to Douglas Gibson, May 29, 1987

Reprinted from: Skelton Grant, Judith. For Your Eye Alone.
Toronto: McClelland & Stewart, Penguin Books, 1999.

Dear Douglas,

If my recollection serves me rightly I wrote to thank you for Margaret Drabble's book [The Radiant Way], which I had not at that time read. Since then I have read it, and I am sure you must be proud to have published such a book, which is a remarkable reflection of our times in the U.K. The shadow of Mrs. Thatcher is strong in it, as is also the somewhat naïve revolt against her by people who want "freedom" but would not much like paying the price it would cost if Labour got back in – freedom to be struck against, and exploited by a cynical labour group, and held to ransom by the entrepreneurs and the so-called "workers." (How on earth have they promoted that usage, which suggest that people like you and me do not really work – just trifle our lives away at the Ritz.) I am no Thatcherite, but at present I do not see any other salvation for Britain; her Philistine contempt for the arts and for education gags me, but she seems to be able to salvage the currency and that is a great thing.

But enough of that: I thought the book was the fine thermometer of its time, and consequently the temperature was not always comfortable. It was also very feminist, in a sensible and irresistible way. I was, during April, in Washington for a meeting of writers called The Wheatland Conference on Literature, financed by the Gettys; unlike most literary conferences I have attended, it made sense, was intelligently small – about fifty people – and had a firm program for discussion. Everybody had a chance to speak. There I met Margaret Drabble with her husband Michael Holroyd, whom I had already met. No question about who leads the band in *that* marriage. Now I shall tell you a story about Holroyd I heard from a very good source in London last autumn: the day before he was about to be married he confided this fact to his mistress; she made a scene; he was astonished; "But I thought you would be delighted to be on the periphery of my happiness!" said he. There's a complexity of sensibility for you! I liked him but he seems utterly subsumed in his book on Shaw, which has been ten years in the making; I think he likes leaving all the decision-making to Miss D. I liked Miss D. too, but somewhat feared her, for she had absolutely not one scrap of humour about her, and in conversation one had to be careful not to make jokes, or one would be greeted with a look of incomprehension – and I respect her too much to insult her by explaining a joke. Talked a bit about the *Oxford Companion*, a queer compilation in which rather too many contemporaries appear and too many oldies have been dropped. But God forbid that I should ever have to make such choices!

We must get together and exchange gossip. But at present I am over my head in my latest novel [The Lyre of Orpheus], which completes the trilogy begun with Angels and What's Bred; it is a complex book but I must not make it too complex or ride my hobbies too hard – a fault for which some grave Western critics[1] have been scolding me recently. I am also the subject of a Twayne book by one Michael Peterman of Trent University; he is down on me for all the old things – elitist, given to big words, sloppy construction, too found of improbable (unPetermanlike) characters, can't draw women, and flawed, flawed, flawed. All written in the kind of Quaker Oats prose one expects of a Peterborough academic. But I suppose I am an old lion and the asses want to skin me and hee-haw in my shrunken skin.

I hope life goes well with you and that your wife is restored to full health.

For the moment, farewell –

Rob.

---

[1] See Robertson Davies's letter of April 20, 1987 (*For Your Eye Alone* pp. 178-179).

Letter from Robertson Davies to Douglas Gibson, March 25

Dear Douglas,

Herewith the typescript of *Murther and Walking Spirits* which now embodies many of your suggestions and alterations. Not all, for I thought some of them needless, and some inadvisable, because I sense that your notion of the novel is different from mine; you have edited always for a rigorous clarity, and I feel that a certain fuzziness is essential to the nature of the book which is, after all, about a man whose perceptions are not those of ourselves. This also a part of the reliance on a film presentation of the narrator's past, for film presents itself to us as photographic – and the camera cannot lie – but is in fact extremely selective and often downright duplicitous in what it offers; Christine [Pevitt[2]] asked that this be given a clearer statement, and I have rewritten the last two-pages of Chapter One to meet this criticism, and they are in the script now.

Kicking and screaming as I wrote, I have shoehorned another generation into the Gage-Vermuelen family, to meet your objection that everybody lived too long; I did not feel when I was writing that a statistical realism was needed, but you do, and now you've got it, though it creates a lump in the narrative that I do not like. I agree with Christine, however, that a family tree would be a mistake; it encourages people to think of the book as one of those sweating family narratives – *The Hoogows of Dogmess: A Saga* – which it is not. Strip aside all my mists, and you kill the book.

Because I have incorporated all the changes directly on the pages, the typescript is not as tidy as I – or Moira Whalon, who takes great pride in such things – could wish. But I think it is clear, and if you or anybody concerned finds my writing difficult, I can explain by phone.

Here and there, my comments on your criticism are a little saucy – a protest against a too-literal reading. Do not take it personally.

I welcome enquiries, protests, loud screams, or whatever.

Rob. Davies

---

[2] Christine Pevitt: (1945-) British senior vice president and publisher at Viking Penguin in New York and Robertson Davies's editor there (1988-91).

About the Douglas Gibson Books Imprint

Douglas Gibson Books was the very first editorial imprint in Canada when it was established in March 1986. Legend has it that Jack McClelland, having just sold his company to Avie Bennett, advised him to lure Doug Gibson away from Macmillan of Canada, where he had been Editorial Director since 1974 and Publisher since 1979. By offering Gibson an editorial imprint, plus the independence to run what was in effect a one-man publishing house with no bureaucratic strings attached, Bennett was able to entice him to join McClelland & Stewart.

The hope was that some of the authors who had worked with Gibson over the years would choose to join him in this small "boutique" publishing operation, where he took on only 5-10 books per year and devoted himself to hands-on editing, choosing the jacket and all other details, and supervising the book through the publishing process.

The plan worked brilliantly. The authors who chose to follow Gibson from Macmillan were led by Alice Munro (*The Progress of Love* in 1986 was the very first Douglas Gibson Book.) Soon the parade of authors included W.O. Mitchell, Robertson Davies, Jack Hodgins, Donald Jack, Mavis Gallant and so many others that Macmillan in a few years folded its fiction publishing programme. The addition of authors such as these to M&S's own already strong fiction list made for a very formidable group of fiction writers.

In non-fiction the list soon included John Sawatsky, Andy Russell, Barry Broadfoot, Myrna Kostash and Harold Horwood, among many others. Notable among the new additions was Don Starkell, author of the classic Paddle to the Amazon, while over time James' Houston (*Memoirs of an Igloo Dweller*, and other titles) and Peter Gzowski (*The Private Voice*, and other titles) asked to join the imprint.

In September 1988, when Adrienne Clarkson left M&S, Avie Bennett persuaded Gibson to take over as Publisher of all McClelland & Stewart books. The wide-ranging new responsibilities meant that Douglas Gibson Books turned into a side-line. As a result Gibson devoted evening and weekend work to three or four books a year, largely because current Douglas Gibson Books authors expected and wanted the relationship to continue.

Despite this cut-back in numbers, Douglas Gibson Books has over the years amassed many prizes, including Governor-General's Awards and Giller Prizes, and many of the titles remain in print year after year, as the list below demonstrates.

Since 1988 Gibson has kept the annual list very small. To avoid any conflict of interest with his role at M&S he encouraged many former authors to join the main M&S list, notably people like Ken Dryden, Guy Vanderhaeghe, Maggie Siggins, Robert Hunter, Michele Landsberg, Jeffrey Simpson and Roy MacGregor.

On occasion he edited M&S books without adding them to his personal imprint. Notable examples are the Memoirs of Pierre Trudeau and Alistair MacLeod's books, No Great Mischief and Island.

In 2004, he returned to his imprint full-time as publisher of Douglas Gibson Books, which now publishes five to ten books a year. The imprint continues to represent Gibson's eclectic personal interests in politics, history, biography, high adventure, and fine fiction.

Introduction to Hugh MacLennan's Best

Reprinted with the permission of the author

This book is a tribute to Hugh MacLennan. I have approached its creation as a friend of Hugh's for more than twenty years as his editor and publisher, and as a staunch admirer of his work in all of its surprising variety. My chief hope for this anthology is that it will give its readers such enjoyment that they will be inspired to read – or re-read – all of the books briefly presented here.

In making this anthology I had the pleasure of reading everything that Hugh MacLennan published, and much that has never been published in book form. I received helpful advice and suggestions from many people, whom I list in the Acknowledgements. At the end of the process, I found myself pleasantly troubled by an embarrassment of riches. To the reader disappointed not to find here a favourite passage from one of the novels, or incredulous that an essentially delightful essay is missing, I apologize for the exclusion. To anthologize is to choose, and here the choosing was hard. In fact, I have come to regret that I have only one book to devote to this marvelous writer.

"This marvelous writer." That phrase is untypical of the editorial style in the rest of the book. There, my role has been to introduce each piece with a brief sentence or two, perhaps referring to the events of MacLennan's life at the time or to similar passages elsewhere, then to leave the excerpt – without benefit of adjectives – to speak for itself.

This introduction, then, may be the place to throw away such reticence (so characteristic of Hugh MacLennan himself) and to speak of his contribution to our national literature. Margaret Lawrence, who was almost uniquely qualified to comment, has written: "MacLennan was our first truly non-colonial writer, writing faithfully out if his own perceptions of his land and his people. In this way, his writing has reached beyond geographical boundaries, and belongs both to Canada and to a universal area of literature. His books will endure."

Others recognized his central role as a pioneer who showed by his example that to be a Canadian novelist was a noble calling. Let one personal anecdote serve as an illustration. I remember the winter day when he delivered the manuscript of *Voices in Time* to me at the Château de Versailles in Montreal, where a committee of the Writer's Union of Canada was meeting. I insisted that he drop in to say hello to this group of a dozen senior Canadian authors, and after much persuasion, because he was reluctant to disturb them, he went in shyly. Everyone in the room stood up and applauded.

This book is for those who would like to know what he did to earn that applause, as well as for his already wide audience of admirers.

Claude Bissell of the University of Toronto, one admirer, has made the flat assertion, "No Canadian writer has contributed so much to national self-awareness and understanding." It is extraordinary now to recollect that when Hugh MacLennan wrote *Barometer Rising* in 1941, it was regarded as an act of almost foolhardy courage to set a novel in Canada. But with that book and with *Two Solitudes*, the 1945 novel that gave every caring Canadian a new expression to ponder, Hugh MacLennan was in the forefront of hacking out a path to a national literature. And his later novels, from *The Watch That Ends the Night*, which held me spellbound as a schoolboy in Scotland reading of Jerome Martell's escape down the river from the lumber camp to *Voices in Time*, whose Portuguese edition confronts me as I write today, have touched hundreds of thousands of readers here and abroad.

But even that is only part of Hugh MacLennan's contribution – he will be remembered with gratitude as a teacher, a generous adviser, a caring husband, a man for whom the word "courtly" might have been invented, and as a friend to many, including writers of all generations. As an essayist he has been among the world's best, writing excellent and much-quoted pieces on everything from hockey to Captain Bligh. Some of those essays reflect his unmatched skills as a writer about the Canadian landscape – gloriously demonstrated here in the short excerpts from *The Colour of Canada* or the longer ones from *Rivers of Canada*, and in the wonderful, much quoted opening to *Two Solitudes*. Like his novels, the essays reveal him as a writer *engagé*, a writer dealing with vital political issues. Hugh MacLennan was notable for his willingness to tackle the great themes, the questions that shape our lives to this day. He was writing about French and English relations in Canada in 1945. As early as 1960, he was writing essays about what he called "the Americanization of Canada." It is worth recalling here that it was MacLennan's essays that taught the American critic Edmund Wilson that there was indeed "a Canadian way of looking at things... a point of view surprisingly and agreeably different from anything else I know in English."

That "Canadian way of looking at things" is a very personal one and the things Hugh MacLennan looks at in this book are so varied that we are left feeling with some awe that he can write well about anything under the sun. His unrivalled record of five Governor General's Awards – three for fiction, and two for his non-fiction essay collections – remind us of his extraordinary range.

He can write about a funny encounter with a trigger-happy barfly in Arizona, and link it with 16th-century religious debates in England. He can describe the torture chambers of the Gestapo, or the eerie shuffling of the homeless Kulaks in Leningrad, and also write a ribald story about Cape Breton nicknames. He can take us to sunny Wimbledon, or to a steamy New Jersey arena by night. And just as deftly he can write about chopping wood in his beloved Eastern Townships.

At the same time he can make Canada and its history spring to life in our senses: he can make us see the yellow foam above the Fraser in flood at Hell's Gate; hear the bagpipes blowing as Sir George Simpson's giant Hudson's Bay canoe is paddled to the Lakehead; feel the impact of the Halifax explosion – or of Jerome Martell's bayonet stuck in the German soldier's throat; or smell the scent of new-mown hay in St. Marc in *Two Solitudes*.

And, of course, he can make us laugh. The fact that his novels have serious themes has blinded too many people to the fact that he is very funny indeed. "Orgy at Oriel," several other essays included here, and many episodes in his novels make that abundantly clear. In his life he was good company, a fine amusing story-teller. I hope that this selection will provide the reader with that same sense of enjoyment.

The organization of this book is very simple. Starting with excerpts from MacLennan's earliest work, the book moves chronologically to the latest work. The editor's role is to introduce each piece briefly in the hope that the chronological arrangement will show how Hugh MacLennan's writing developed. In that way this book may perhaps be seen as a useful companion volume to Elspeth Cameron's excellent biography, *Hugh MacLennan: A Writer's Life* (University of Toronto Press, 1981).

Usually the excerpt is four or five pages long. Sometimes it is self-contained: an essay; a description of a river from Rivers of Canada; an incident from a novel; a memorable scene described in a way that reveals one of the many facets of the author's skill.

When Hugh MacLennan died in November 1990, editorials in newspaper across the country mourned Canada's loss. Some paid tribute to his ability, as one who had lived in every decade of this most turbulent of centuries, to notice and call attention to the important movements in our world. Others spoke of his pioneering role in creating a literature that belonged to Canada, and recalled Robert Kroetsch's poetic description of Hugh MacLennan as "the cartographer of our dreams."

At the end of this book, I hope that everyone will feel as David Helwig did after reading his essays:

"MacLennan is one of those writers whose personal goodness and decency shine through all his works. His generosity of spirit is such that after a couple of hours spent with one of his books, the world seems a better place."

Douglas Gibson

Toronto, June 1991

ANNEX 4

Call me "A Superb and Totally Objective Editor"
Doug Gibson

*Reprinted with the permission of the author
and* Quill and Quire *Magazine*

I've had an unusual, possibly unique, experience this spring as I edited my books for this fall. Two of the non-fiction works contain among the cast of characters an editor and publisher named Doug Gibson. Me. As others see me.

The others in this case are Robert Thacker, the author of *Alice Munro: Writing Her Lives, a Biography*, and the husband-and-wife team Orm and Barbara Mitchell who are completing their biography of W.O. Mitchell with a second volume entitled *Mitchell: the Life of W. O. Mitchell. The Years of Fame, 1948 to 1998*.

My involvement with Alice runs from 1975 to the present and includes nine books (and counting), while I worked with W.O. from 1975 till his death in 1998, a period that saw us produce together nine titles, so the biographer's files on me are full, and I crop up in each story with alarming frequency.

It all began badly with the research interviews. It should be understood that any biographer immersed in research is an obsessive, a sort of licensed fanatic. They know what their subject had for breakfast on March 12, 1979 and if you were at the table they know what you ate – or they expect you to remember. I thought that I had a fairly good memory until their tape recorders went on. It was humiliating.

"In summer 1986 you were really angry," says Bob Thacker.

"I was?"

"You remember the trouble you had getting the Alex Colville painting for the cover of *The Progress of Love* from the Art Gallery of Ontario?"

"No – but usually we need the image faster than galleries are used to working. I'm sure there wasn't anything special about it."

103

"Doug – you set the lawyers on them."

"I did?"

And so on. If this had happened in open court I would have been the very model of an evasive witness, prime material for a Gomery Commission hot seat.

The Mitchells were equally demanding on my memory. They had a detailed question about how W.O. and I chose the order for the stories in *According to Jake and the Kid.* They knew that on such and such a day W.O. and Merna came to Toronto and the stories were placed in order. I remembered the circumstances, dealing the stories like giant cards on to W.O.'s hotel bedspread and finding that we were in such instant agreement that it was all done in less than 20 minutes.

"Yes, yes," they probed. "But why did you choose that order?"

"Well, you know, you start and end with a strong story then, um, you try to mix up the long and short stories and, er, the funny ones and the more serious ones and (feebly) try to end up with, um, an order that works."

They looked away, disappointed.

And so it went. Question after question was answered with "I just can't recall" and "I'm sorry, I can't remember," until I realized that if I'd been on trial any sensible juror would have found me guilty, recommending the maximum sentence, with perjury charges thrown in.

So when the manuscripts arrived, I should not have been surprised to learn that these authors knew a lot more about my life since roughly 1975 than I did. As it was, I'm shocked to learn that this fellow Gibson had led a far from blameless life.

Here's Gibson being reprimanded by his bosses at Macmillan for failing to follow normal channels when signing up Alice Munro's father's manuscript as part of what Thacker calls "the wooing process." Here he is consistently misspelling W.O.'s wife's name in letters intended to gain the redoubtable Merna's approval: what a moron. Here Gibson is stupidly neglecting to inform Alice Munro's agent about his far-advanced publishing plans for *Who Do You Think You Are,* and trying to avoid war through a mollifying letter that admits blame and concludes, "let's be friends." Here he is, notoriously holding Alice to her responsibility to pay for excessive author changes at a late stage of the proofs. Here he is delaying a response to a part-manuscript by W.O. until the Mitchell household is convinced (wrongly) that he doesn't like it. And here's Gibson clearly losing his temper with protracted contract negotiations on a book actually at the printer and breaking all kinds of agent protocols to contact W.O. directly "to cut through all the nonsense" (a phrase that does have a familiar ring to it).

Oh dear.

Yet, predictably, over the course of 30 years and so many books together with Alice, and with W.O., the character named Gibson seemed to do some things right. His affection for W.O. and Merna and their feisty marriage sustained by "the power of mutual recrimination" (did I really say that?) comes through loud and clear. And there are pleasing reminders of long-forgotten battles fought on W.O.'s or Alice's behalf. There is even the letter to Alice from September 1980, also long-forgotten, that reads well today: "but keep in mind the assurance that I gave you some years ago. I'm not going to pester you to write novels. I'm perfectly pleased to go on publishing collections of Alice Munro stories – related or unrelated – as long as you keep writing them."

And a wonderful bonus was discovering, for the first time, the letters that Alice wrote to Macmillan in 1986, explaining why she valued my help and wanted to follow me with *The Progress of Love* to the new Douglas Gibson Books imprint being established at M&S.

But how do you edit this stuff? My approach was the predictable, indeed only sensible one, to treat Doug Gibson as just another character like Ginger Barber or Merna Mitchell. So I can clean up some of Gibson's clumsy direct quotes, but only to the extent that I'm removing the same "you know" from other quotes. And I will, and have, cut Gibson's quotes or quotes about him just as ruthlessly as other surplus quotes. And so on with the authors as witnesses to, even referees of, the evenhandedness of the system, with the reader as the ultimate arbiter.

As the editing process proceeds, it's proving to be interesting, and seems to be working well enough. I did, of course, make the suggestion that the first time Gibson makes an appearance in the book the name should be followed by the parenthetical description, "whose striking good looks and stunning intelligence are matched only by his excessive modesty." So far, disappointingly, it hasn't shown up. But as every old publishing pro knows, it's amazing what can happen at the printers.

Alligators in the Sewers:
Publishing Alistair MacLeod
By Douglas Gibson

*Reprinted with the permission of the author. First printed in Alistair
MacLeod, Essays On His Works. Edited by Irene Guilford,
published by Guernica Editions, Toronto, 1992*

Modern urban legends spring out of everywhere and nowhere. We all
know for a fact that a cement truck operator avenged himself on the man
who was dallying with the trucker's wife by filling his Mercedes with
wet cement. And we thrill to the knowledge that some of our cities now
have a flourishing alligator population deep in the warm sewers, the
offsping of the little baby gators flushed away by bored owners unaware
of the subterranean monsters they were creating.

Alistair MacLeod and I have been living in the midst of such an urban myth. As it spins more wildly out of control, we compare notes,
bemused by the directions the myth takes, aware that we seem to be in
the grip of something bigger than both of us. The once-simple story of
how I encouraged Alistair to finish the novel that became *No Great
Mischief* has taken the following turns. In Nova Scotia legend has me
flying to Halifax then driving to Cape Breton (soon, presumably, it will
be in a storm, with the closed Canso causeway, under water, proving no
obstacle to the wild-eyed publisher) and then, rushing on foot to Alistair's writing cabin to wrest the manuscript from his grasp. Even in
Ontario, the range of stories can make a reader dizzy. Sometimes the
manuscript is exchanged for a bottle of whiskey in Union Station.
Sometimes the exciting new versions involve my driving to Windsor
dashing into the office of Professor MacLeod and grabbing a manuscript
written by hand on exam paper notebooks. Best of all is the story first
aired in the *National Post* and then passed along by the *Edmonton
Journal* – a story very popular in the halls of McClelland & Stewart –
where the delivery of the manuscript's final chapter at the M&S office
causes me to burst into tears of relief.

Alistair has perfected the art of being non-committal about such stories, perhaps a legacy of his years as a creative writing teacher reluctant to stamp out any fictional spark. Presumably by the time this account sees the light of day the legend will have expanded in other directions, possibly involving parachutes and guns.

The true story is as follows. Alistair published both his short story collections *The Lost Salt Gift of Blood* (1976) and *As Birds Bring Forth the Sun* (1986) with McClelland & Stewart. I became M&S's publisher in 1988, but of course knew Alistair's work. Indeed, I had got to know him in person at the Banff Centre where he worked as a much admired teacher in the summer with W.O. Mitchell's creative writing programme (itself the source of many stories, not least Alistair's side-splitting account of his winter trip by taxi with W.O. from Calgary to Banff.) And one summer in the mid-1980s, when the Gibson family was touring in the Maritimes, we visited the MacLeods in Dunvegan. Between juvenile soccer games on the grass in front of the house, Alistair showed us around his corner of Cape Breton and I remember walking that grassy track to his Spartan cliff-top writing cabin, which faces west to Prince Edward Island. It struck me at the time that, with the sound of the wind and the waves and the constantly changing view, I would get very little writing done there.

As McClelland & Stewart's publisher I was in the happy position of having inherited Alistair, and so from 1988 was appropriately interested in how his work was coming along. Over the years, as it became clear that the work he had started in 1986 was a novel, and as Alistair's readings from the novel at events across the country produced a groundswell of excitement, my contact would consist of a cheery phone call every six months or so, asking how the writing was going. This would produce charmingly vague responses from the Windsor (or, in the summer, the Cape Breton) end of the line. So vague, in fact, that I would rely on information from a friend in the M&S warehouse, a member of Alistair's extended family, for reports on his progress. There were many other friends and admirers, "MacLeod-watchers" (like Kremlin-watchers in the old days who would read significance into the arrangements of Soviet officials on a reviewing stand), who would pass on scraps of information about what he had read at this event, or mentioned about his manuscript in that interview or meeting.

All the while, of course, Alistair was holding down a demanding job teaching English and Creative Writing at Windsor (to the great benefit of his appreciative students), teaching a summer course at Banff, and raising six children with Anita, not to mention undertaking annual family moves between Windsor and Cape Breton. So I did not feel able to harass the man beyond the point of regular encouraging phone calls, letting him know that there was continuing interest at M&S, and in the wider world, in his next book.

This changed around the beginning of 1999. All of my "how's it coming along" questions – which Alistair has accurately likened to the "are we there yet?" questions from the kids in the back seat on a long car trip – had extracted no hard information about what proportion of the manuscript was now written. The book, despite my repeated offers, was still not under contract, presumably because Alistair was reluctant to commit to a specific delivery. But messages from the "MacLeod-watchers" and my own sense of his situation led me to step up the pressure. My main motive was commercial. I could see that very few of the major figures in Canadian literature would have a new book in the fall of 1999 – Alice Munro had appeared the previous year, Margaret Atwood, Michael Ondaatje, Rohinton Mistry and Jane Urquhart, among others, were not due for another year at least – so a book by a respected but not widely-known author like Alistair MacLeod would have a chance to rise to the top, would have, to change the metaphor, room to breathe.

So my phone calls became more frequent, and more urgent, especially after Alistair rashly allowed that it was possible that he might finish the book in time for fall publication. I have referred to him as a stone-carver, chipping out each perfect word with loving care. Certainly my confidence in the excellence of his writing was such that – without having read a word of the manuscript – I felt able to put the book in the Fall 1999 catalogue (going to the printer at the end of May) and to write him a letter in April outlining very precisely the generous terms we would offer for the new book, for which we would hold "a place of honour" in our fall list.

In the midst of this campaign of harassment, I learned that Alistair would be reading in Toronto. Unluckily, I had a previous engagement in Ottawa at the opening of a James Houston-inspired show of Inuit Art at the Museum of Civilization that same evening. But the next day I flew back early from Ottawa, and called Anita in Windsor to announce that I really wanted to see her husband while he was in Toronto. She told me where he was staying and mentioned that he was catching the 4:30 train back to Windsor. Failing to catch him before he checked out, I decided, with our Chairman Avie Bennett's amused encouragement, to try a direct approach.

So it came about that the unfortunate Dr. MacLeod, peacefully reading a book in Union Station at 4:00, found a bearded man in a coat dropping down to sit beside him on the bench with the words: "Isn't this amazing! Here I am patrolling Union Station in search of a best-selling novel for this fall, and I happen to run into you!"

We laughed, but I was able to emphasize the urgency of the matter, in person, and to tell him how certain I was that the literary world was eagerly awaiting this book (something that Alistair, a truly modest man, found hard to believe, even though I assured him that I was right on this.) Above all, I was able to urge him on to a final sprint as he approached the finish line of this long distance race. Alistair was politely non-committal. When the Windsor train was called and a queue began to form there was a fine moment when I offered to carry his briefcase, with a look of frank, open-hearted generosity, and Alistair laughed and clutched the bag protectively to his chest. Laughing, but still clutching.

To keep the pressure on, I put the book in the M&S catalogue, writing a description of the novel that stands up remarkably well, given that I had not yet read a word of it, or learned more than a sentence or two about it from the tight lips of the author. (When the manuscript later came in, containing the two lines of poetry that immediately preceded the two lines I had chosen to quote in the catalogue, I knew the gods were with us.)

At this point the title changed. It had originally been *No Great Mischief If They Fall*, but Alistair phoned to report that he had just learned of a Scottish book with the same title. Not necessarily a problem, I said, since titles are not restricted by copyright. "Ah well," said Alistair, "unfortunately, the name of the other book's author is MacLeod." In one second the book became *No Great Mischief*, as nature surely intended.

As we neared the end of May the pressure on both of us increased. The catalogue was about to be printed at the end of the month, and it is not good for a book to be announced and then postponed. My phone calls about needing to see the manuscript by mid-May were not bearing fruit. Finally, on a Wednesday I called Windsor to tell Alistair that, because we were nearing catalogue deadline and because our sales conference was the following Tuesday and I could not face 40 or 50 people and describe the merits of a book I had not read, I was flying down to Windsor on Friday to pick up the manuscript.

He was appalled. No, no, it wasn't ready, I shouldn't do that, and so on. But I told him I was coming, hung up, and didn't answer my phone for two days. At the airport on Friday morning, while my office was calling Alistair to let him know I was indeed on my way, I ran into Heather Robertson, the well-known author, who asked me where I was going and was fascinated to hear about my mission. (One year later Heather was to be part of the jury that unanimously gave the Trillium Prize to *No Great Mischief*.) Arriving in Windsor, I startled the cab driver by asking to be taken to the nearest liquor store. He swung around nervously, checking for indications that I would pass out, or worse, throw up, on this back seat. Then, armed with a bottle of Talisker, a fine malt from the appropriate part of the Highlands, I went on to the MacLeod house.

At the door, I received a courteous but reserved reception from Alistair, and I was glad to have the Talisker to present. And we sat in the front room with Anita and chatted for a bit about our families, and it was very pleasant. But there was an elephant in the room that we were all ignoring. After all, I had barged into their lives with the express intention of wresting the manuscript out of his hands. To make matters worse, no manuscript was in view. Much worse, above the piano I could see the MacLeod clan coat of arms with its terrible, blood-chilling motto: "Hold fast."

I did not comment on this.

Eventually, I produced a contract for the book and laid the large envelope on the coffee table, noting that they should treat it with care because it also contained a cheque, and then wondered aloud what he had for me. And Alistair rose in silence and left the room – *and came back carrying a manuscript!* Needless to say, it never left my possession from that moment until I was back in Toronto, jubilant from having read a wonderful piece of literature.

But not, it proved, a complete one. After Alistair had taken me to lunch downtown (and significantly he was greeted in the parking lot *and* outside the restaurant *and* by another diner in the restaurant) and told me about the book's plot for the first time, he drove me to his office at the University. I noticed many hand-written scraps of paper. In response to my question, Alistair admitted that he wrote long-hand and the absence of secretarial help in summer vacation time meant that his final chapters were being held up while he asked others to type it for him as a favour. I reeled at the thought of this bottleneck and promptly arranged for him to send his remaining hand-written chapters to us by courier and we would arrange to get them typed and on a disc.

And so, for the next six weeks or so, a package of 10 or 12 or 15 pages written by hand on yellow paper would arrive every few days at the M&S office, and I would take it for typesetting to two young interns, Medbh Bidwell and Adrienne Guthrie, graduates of the Simon Fraser University Masters programme in publishing. They were initially a little hesitant about this menial typing assignment, although I assured them that they were playing a role in Canadian literary history: they soon came to agree, as their wonder at the material they were typing grew along with their impatience to find out what happened next. My reaction to the final chapter was misunderstood by the *National Post* and the *Edmonton Journal* but will be easily grasped by anyone who reads the book and its last line: "All of us are better when we are loved." I was moved to tears.

My role in editing the book was almost non-existent. The early material, typed in a variety of faces over the years, was so polished that it needed almost no attention from me. Alistair's style is distinctive – sparse punctuation, a frequent preference for "which" instead of "that," much use of "perhaps," and dialogue punctuated very simply by "he said" so that a variant "expostulated" would bring the whole chapter crashing down – and it is so deliberate and the rhythms so clear that pages if the manuscript would fly by untouched by editorial hand.

On occasion my own Scottish background (I was born and raised there, leaving St. Andrews University with a scholarship that took me across the Atlantic) proved to be very useful. For example, I knew a lot about Montrose's rebellion, having played the role of Montrose in a St. Andrews' procession – cavalier's hat, breastplate, sword, thigh-boots and all (not to mention the runaway horse) – so I was able to clarify the odd historical detail. By way of general helpfulness I was able, for example, to remind Alistair of Eliot's lines about Rannoch Moor when he was describing that area, and I was sound in the general area of Scottish history and, by extension, the battles at Beauport and upstream on the Plains of Abraham. (And if you shake your head at the ubiquity of Scots in Canada, consider that the aforementioned Abraham was "Abraham Martin, dit l'Écossais.")

Another Scottish aside: Rannoch Moor is where Alan Breck Stewart and David Balfour spent a hot day being hunted by English redcoats in *Kidnapped*. Robert Louis Stevenson, who knew something about Jekyll and Hyde personalities, has been credited with making these two characters represent the two sides of what might be called the Scottish schizophrenic personality: David, the sober, plodding, industrious common-sense Presbyterian Lowlander (good material for lawyers, bankers, engineers and doctors), and Alan Breck, the wild, creative, romantic Highlander, an ideal man to set up a new fur trade route, to conquer a kingdom, to cry over a sad song or to fight in wars around the world. Working with Alistair – a Highlander to the bone – it was hard not to find myself being tugged into the ethnic role of my Lowland ancestors. In terms of the historic events of the book, these ancient Gibsons were presumably all in favour of Bruce (another Ayrshire man) and Bannockburn, where they were on the same side as the MacDonalds; but they were opposed to Montrose, dead set against "Bonnie Dundee" ("Bloody Claverhouse") at Killiecrankie, and notably unenthusiastic about Bonnie Prince Charlie. Now, centuries later and a world away, here I was, David Balfour-like, urging the commercial advantages of finishing a novel like a sober man of business, on Alistair, a Celtic visionary and a great artist. It was, and is, a sobering thought.

Understandably, I was useless as an editor when it came to Gaelic. A toast, a greeting, a few swear words, enough topographical features to be able to tell a Ben from a Loch, that was the extent of my knowledge, although I grew up in an Ayrshire village with a Gaelic name. So I called on the assistance of a husband and wife team from Scotland, now in Toronto, and they raised a number of proof-reading questions that Anita (the expert in the household) was able to settle. By the end I was familiar enough with the language that, to my great satisfaction, I caught a typo in the Gaelic dedication.

The expert copy-editor, Heather Sangster, maintained the same light-handed editorial approach, recognizing that the deliberately oral way of story-telling adopted by the author right from the start ("as most people hearing this will know" – page 3) called for deliberate repetition of certain phrases, such as "the modernistic house in Calgary." As always, such a skilled copy-editor caught inconsistencies that had somehow escaped the eyes of both author and editor over many readings.

In terms of the text, my chief role was to work with the designer to produce a book page that did justice to the writing. The typeface is clean, traditional and easy to read, with plenty of "leading" space between lines. There are 43 chapters in the 283 pages of *No Great Mischief* so to start each new chapter on a fresh page would make the book seem padded. Hence our decision to allow a six-line spacing between chapters, and to mark each chapter opening simply with a numeral set against a Celtic design.

The book was not divided into formal chapters when it came to my office. I consulted Alistair by phone and undertook to divide it into chapters as seemed best to me, with occasional one-line breaks in the middle of a chapter when something less that a full chapter break seemed appropriate (see page 181, for one example). I am happy to report that when we first saw the proofs of the book, formally divided into chapters, Alistair and I agreed that I had got it right the first time, with the exception of one paragraph, which was moved back into the preceding chapter.

After that it was merely a matter of giving the book and appropriate look, which our Kong Njo, in his role as Art Director, did with his usual skill (tactfully ignoring my suggestion that the MacDonald tartan might show up somewhere on the cover. Incidentally, at a Cape Breton launch for the book, the hall was decorated in the MacLeod and MacDonald tartans, no to mention variants of the McClelland and Stewart tartans.

Had this particular Gibson been able to be present, the Buchanan tartan might also have put in an appearance).

In the course of presenting the book to our Sales Conference, that famous conference in June 1999, I did something unprecedented. I used music to convey the sense of the book. To be precise, from my "Puirt à Baroque" recording, I played "Niel Gow's Lament" in the background while I talked about how the music of the Scottish Highlands and of Cape Breton pervades this marvellous book. And the sad, slow music of the fiddle was worth a thousand words.

The publishing success of *No Great Mischief* is history, and it is history that is being written around the world, with publishers in a dozen other countries engaged in revealing the wonders of the book to their readers. A special pleasure for me was seeing the success of *No Great Mischief* as early as October and consequently urging Alistair to let us publish his collected short stories in the spring. There have been very few criticisms of any aspect of the novel but some critics have complained that the dialogue in Alistair's work does not sound realistic to their ears. My reply is that they have never talked much with Alistair MacLeod.

As far as I can reconstruct it, the conversation went as follows:

"Alistair," I said. "Would you have any other stories besides the fourteen that are in the two story collections?"

"Yes," He said, "I would."

"And how many do you have?"

"I have two," he said.

"And what are their names?"

"One is called 'Island' and the other is called 'Clearances.'"

"And are they short or long?"

"Oh, they are both quite long."

"Well," I said, "in the spring we will bring out a book of your collected short stories and we will call it either *Island* or *Clearances*. And we will do very well with it."

"Do you think so?"

"Oh yes," I said. "And I have been right before."

And we both laughed.

Douglas Gibson's Biography

(From the M&S website)

Douglas Maitland Gibson was born in 1943 and raised in Scotland, where he gained an MA at the University of St. Andrews. After acquiring a further MA at Yale, he came to Canada in 1967 and entered the world of publishing in March 1968, as an editor with Doubleday Canada. Through a series of accidents he found himself running an editorial department at the age of 25, and publishing books set from Newfoundland (Death on the Ice, by Cassie Brown) to British Columbia (Vancouver, by Eric Nicol) and editing authors ranging from Harry J. Boyle (The Great Canadian Novel) to Barry Broadfoot (Ten Lost Years.)

He joined Macmillan of Canada as Editorial Director in 1974 and became Publisher in 1979. In those years he had the privilege of editing authors such as Morley Callaghan, Hugh MacLennan, Bruce Hutchison, and Robertson Davies. Early in 1986 he joined McClelland & Stewart as Editor and Publisher of a new line of books under his own imprint, a first in Canada. Since then Douglas Gibson Books has published works by authors such as Alice Munro, Peter Gzowski, Jack Hodgins, James Houston, W.O. Mitchell and Mavis Gallant. In September, 1988 the Douglas Gibson Books line was reduced to three titles a year when he became Publisher of McClelland & Stewart, overseeing all of its books and attracting to the house many former associates, including Robertson Davies, Ken Dryden, Myrna Kostash, Jeffrey Simpson, Michele Landsberg, Roy MacGregor and Guy Vanderhaeghe. In June 2000 he became President and Publisher of McClelland & Stewart.

As an old friend of Hugh MacLennan, he was one of four eulogists at his funeral in Montreal in 1990. A year later the anthology Hugh MacLennan's Best, "selected and edited by Douglas Gibson," was published, and in 1994 he contributed to the University of Ottawa Press book Hugh MacLennan. He edited the anthology The Merry Heart; Selections 1980-1995 by Robertson Davies one year after Professor Davies' death, and he has since published posthumous books by his friend W.O. Mitchell.

As a member of the publishing community he has taught courses in editing to many groups, including the Book Publishers' Professional Association and EAC, and contributed the title chapter to the booklet "Author and Editor." From its creation in 1981 he was a Faculty Advisor to the Banff Publishing Workshop, and from 1985 to 1989 was the Co-Director of the course. He was the Chair of the Advisory Board of the Canadian Centre for Studies in Publishing at Simon Fraser University from 1988-1993 and is now an Honorary Advisory Board Member, and an adjunct faculty member for the Master of Publishing program at S.F.U. In 1995 he delivered the annual Hugh MacLennan Lecture at McGill University. He is a member of the Quadrangle Society of Massey College, and the Scottish Studies Board at the University of Guelph.

As a writer, his work has appeared in the anthology, *The Bumper Book*, in a book on Alistair MacLeod and in Saturday Night, Toronto Life, Books in Canada, the National Post and the Globe and Mail, and one of his pieces was nominated for a National Magazine Award for Humour. From 1981 till early in 1984 he was the weekly movie re-viewer for the CBC radio programme "Sunday Morning." In a more serious vein, he has given speeches to groups as varied as the Canadian Oral History Association, the CNIB, and the Canadian Institute of International Affairs, and he made the keynote speech at the Ottawa press conference in 1987 that launched the campaign "Don't Tax Read-ing." He spoke as a Canadian representative at the International Publish-ers' Association Convention in London in 1988. As a Council Member of Historica he has spoken at a number of Canadian Clubs.

In 1991 he received the rarely-presented Canadian Booksellers' As-sociation President's Award "for the numerous important Canadian books and authors he has developed over the years." Since that time his encounters with major M&S books – from The Ice Storm to No Great Mischief, which he extracted from Alistair MacLeod – and with authors ranging from Andy Russell to Toller Cranston and from John Crosbie to Pierre Trudeau, have provided him with material for many speeches across the country.

The year 2005 proved to be a year of awards for Doug Gibson. In April he became the "Canadian Scot of the Year" at a ceremony in Toronto, and in June, at Book Expo, the annual meeting of the book trade in Canada, he received the award "Editor of the Year." This was a very pleasing recognition of his successful return to concentrating on his editorial role once again.

The father of two daughters, he lives in Toronto with his wife, Jane Brenneman Gibson.

Conclusion to this volume

As I finish this work, I happen to come across Alberto Manguel's articles[1] which heavily criticize the very function of editors while I praise Douglas Gibson's work as an editor.

Manguel explains that in the Anglo-Saxon system, and particularly in North America, all manuscripts have to go through the hands of a professional called *editor* in order to stand a chance of being published. Through a couple of anecdotes, Manguel illustrates how editors shamelessly take control over an author's work[2]. These editors do not seem to have official counterparts in France. When we, the French, speak of the *éditeur*, we mean, according to the Robert dictionary either "someone who posts a text," or "a person (or company) who is in charge of the publication and the selling of printed work." These two definitions correspond to the English term of *publisher*. However the distinct responsibilities of the *éditeur* and of the editor do also cover common ground: for example, in both France and Anglo-Saxon countries, the copy-editing of the manuscript is part of the accepted responsibility of the editor. What is put into question by both Manguel and our French editorial culture is the editor's command of the content of the author's work.

When an editor feels entitled to put pressure on the author in such a way that the balance of the work is likely to be upset, the author's creation is potentially in danger. Manguel clearly states out the reason for which North America is typically a greenhouse in which this type of editor thrives: in order to satisfy a mercantile society in which the book is a merchandise like any other, publishing houses hire marketing experts in order to ensure that the books will be produced and sold profitably.

My purpose is not to become a Don Quixote and campaign against the commercial environment in which we live. America has, for some

---

[1] These articles are the following: "Idiot's Fare" *Geist* 63, Winter 2006. pp. 63-66; and: "The Secret Sharer" in *Into the Looking-Glass Wood: Essays on Books, Reading, and the World.* Toronto: Alfred Knopf Canada, 1998. pp. 130-140.

[2] For example, in "The Secret Sharer," Manguel tells the story of Timothy Findley who yields to his editor and sets out to explain the butterfly imagery in *The Butterfly Plague.* In "Idiot's Fare," Manguel quotes Doris Lessing's editor's criticism: "You write too much."

time now, led the way to consumerism – as Tocqueville points out back in the middle of the 19th century[3] – and all capitalist countries follow, as globalisation only increases the speed at which the process is taking place. However, resistance against artistic production for the masses as opposed to quality work, can be found in the search for quality niches. In this enterprise, the editor's role is no longer the one described by Manguel or Gerald Gross in *Editors on Editing*[4].

Although the editor's role is thus not merely limited to producing a clean version of the manuscript, it does not overstep the boundaries of the editorial function according to what we, traditionally, in France, understand this function to be. Indeed, the creation of the work remains the author's sole responsibility and yet, the editor will finds ways of offering a valuable contribution, without interfering in a way which is likely to upset the balance of the work. My interviews with Douglas Gibson allowed me to clarify these possible domains of intervention and I will summarize them here in a couple of points. The editor of quality work is the one who:

- shortlists possibilities and then selects valuable manuscripts;

- encourages the author all the while respecting his need to work on his own;

- looks after the author's work conditions and deals with the material details, allowing the author to focus on the essential;

- "cleans up" the manuscript (copy-edits) without upsetting the creative balance of the work;

---

[3] "La démocratie ne fait pas seulement pénétrer le goût des lettres dans les classes industrielles, elle introduit l'esprit industriel au sein de la littérature." Et : "[C]hez les nations démocratiques, un écrivain peut se flatter d'obtenir à bon marché une médiocre renommée et une grande fortune. Il n'est pas nécessaire pour cela qu'on l'admire, il suffit qu'on le goûte.

La foule toujours croissante des lecteurs et le besoin continuel qu'ils ont du nouveau assurent le débit d'un livre qu'ils n'estiment guère. " Tocqueville (de), Alexis. *De la Démocratie en Amérique, tome 2*. Paris: Garnier-Flammarion, 1981, 51.

[4] Gross, Gerald, *Editors on Editing*, New York, Grove Press, 1993. This volume contains several articles dealing with the editor's role. For example, Gerald Howard comments: "the intersection between culture and commerce where editors do their work is … a sanguine piece of ground." Gerald Howard "Mistah Perkins – He Dead," *Editors on Editing*, New York, Grove Press, 1993, p. 58. This sort of environment encourages anyone with ambition to become a career author, in the following editor's ⌐rms: "Go to the right college, get into the right … program, make the right contacts ¬g established writers and book and magazine editors, find the right literary ⌐ho'll sell your book to the right publisher, who'll give your book the right shake down the right writers … for the right blurbs, and you're off!"

- is in charge of editorial parameters other than the creative content (for example the timing of the publication and launch);

- protects the author from the pitfalls of PR and promotional events;

- finally, and most importantly, to return to the genesis of the work, becomes the author's first attentive reader, thus offering the author the respect he needs to build up more confidence.

A perfect illustration of the superposition of all of these functions is to be found in Douglas Gibson's text entitled "Alligators in the Sewers" where the editor traces back the story of *No Great Mischief*. In this very entertaining account of what led to the publication of a masterpiece, we discover how Douglas Gibson stands by Alistair MacLeod in the last steps of the writing of his work. The blind trust shown by the editor (which Douglas Gibson demonstrates when he puts the novel on the Fall 1999 catalogue without having read one word of the manuscript), as well as the efficient way in which the editor deals with all the material details of the publication (both internally at M&S and externally), bears witness to an editorial skill which is very much opposed to the arrogance described by Manguel, Gross or Howard. Obviously the editor delights in "being along for the ride" as *No Great Mischief* is about to be published – a joy which Douglas Gibson invites everyone to share, including the two interns in charge of typing up the manuscript). And this joy is legitimate enough! But however tempting it may be to pride oneself on having taken a major role in the genesis of the work, Douglas Gibson prefers to state, in his introduction of *No Great Mischief* that he undertook the chapter division task with the author's approval and that the process was an extremely smooth one. Alistair MacLeod's immediate agreement to the chapter divide suggests that Douglas Gibson worked as a passionate reader, and that is he was totally focused on the reading task, all the while conscious of the need to progress according to the established schedule in order to give his author a chance to launch the novel at the most appropriate time.

To finish, I would like to underline how this volume, *Douglas Gibson Unedited*, suggests two distinct areas of discussion and research. As I indicated in my introduction, I hope this work will encourage my university colleagues to dig into the files which Douglas Gibson entrusted to the McMaster University archives.

But although Douglas Gibson definitely holds a unique place as an editor to some of Canada's finest writers, I hope that this volume will reach beyond his individual example in order to raise questions concerning the role of the editor in today's context.

Douglas Gibson exemplifies a form of resistance against the caricatured image of Manguel's *editor*. Indeed, Gibson's experience provides food for thought for all industry players who are conscious of established power structures and commercial pressures at work in today's environment but who nevertheless wish to construct editorial strategies allowing for a maximum of respect for the author's work[5].

My purpose is to highlight the possibility of a resistance against two types of danger – yielding to commercial pressures and to the temptation of total editorial power –, but also I would like to give a glimpse of the incredible joy that lies in the acceptance of a role on the periphery characterized mainly by humility and enthusiasm. As Maxwell Perkins (editor of Fitzgerald and Thomas Wolf), reminds his colleagues: "An editor does not add to a book. At best he serves as a handmaiden to an author. Don't ever get to feeling important about yourself, because an editor at most releases energy. He creates nothing."[6]

It is in line with this philosophy, based on an infinite respect for the author's work, that Douglas Gibson chooses to soldier on, thus encouraging others to do so.

---

[5]   This echoes Gerald Howard's comment: "Yes, the corporate Shenanigans … still go on, the agents call the tune, the culture is decaying, nobody reads anymore, the universe will eventually suffer heat death… Meanwhile, the good editor's task – and there are plenty of good editors out there… – *is simply to ignore all this* and go about the business of bringing the best books he or she can to market, at a price that makes turning a profit possible. This may mean any number of personal and business compromises with a commercial culture capable of the most stupefying inanition. But victories, however difficult to win, are the lifeblood of editors, and they come more often than what one might expect… It means that the soul of publishing, and to a certain extent of American literary and intellectual culture, if that's not too grandiose, resides in the stewardship of editors who care deeply about quality and excellence.

And so we soldier on. And so we'd better." Gerald Howard "Mistah Perkins – He Dead," *Editors on Editing*, New York, Grove Press, 1993, p. 72.

[6]   Berg, A. Scott. *Max Perkins Editor of Genius*. New York: Riverhead Books, 1978, 6.

Conclusion de l'ouvrage

A l'heure où ce travail se termine, je découvre deux articles d'Alberto Manguel qui, au moment même où je fais l'éloge d'un éditeur, critiquent vivement cette fonction dans l'industrie anglo-saxonne du livre[1]. Devant la pertinence des propos de Manguel, je souhaite tenter une réconciliation des deux points de vue.

Manguel explique que dans le système anglo-saxon (et tout particulièrement en Amérique du Nord), tout manuscrit doit passer entre les mains de professionnels appelés *editors* pour avoir la moindre chance d'être publié. Les *editors* s'attribuent un pouvoir que Manguel qualifie d'insensé sur l'œuvre – pouvoir qu'il illustre de plusieurs anecdotes[2]. Les *editors* n'ont pas tout à fait d'équivalent dans le système français. Lorsqu'on parle d'éditeur en France, si l'on se réfère au Robert, on veut dire soit, « Personne qui fait paraître un texte », soit « Personne (ou société) qui assure la publication et la mise en vente d'ouvrages imprimés ». Ces deux définitions renvoient au terme anglais *publisher*. Toutefois, le travail de l'éditeur et celui de l'*editor* recouvrent des fonctions communes : par exemple, en France comme dans le monde anglo-saxon, le « toilettage » de l'œuvre représente une partie reconnue du travail de l'éditeur. Ce qui est davantage contesté, aussi bien par notre culture éditoriale que par Manguel, c'est la prise en charge par l'*editor* de la question du sens de l'œuvre.

Quand l'*editor* exerce une pression susceptible de déranger l'équilibre délicat de la création de l'auteur, l'œuvre est potentiellement en danger. Manguel identifie clairement la raison pour laquelle l'Amérique du Nord est typiquement une serre dans laquelle se développe ce type d'éditeurs : pour satisfaire une société mercantile où le livre est une marchandise comme une autre, les maisons d'édition emploient des experts du marché afin de s'assurer que les livres pourront être produits et écoulés de manière profitable.

---

[1]   Ces articles sont : "Idiot's Fare" *Geist* 63, Winter 2006. pp. 63-66 et "The Secret Sharer" in *Into the Looking-Glass Wood: Essays on Books, Reading, and the World*. Toronto: Alfred Knopf Canada, 1998. pp. 130-140.

[2]   Par exemple, dans "The Secret Sharer," Manguel rapporte l'histoire de Timothy Findley qui se plie à l'exigence de son éditeur pour *The Butterfly Plague* : expliquer l'image des papillons. Dans "Idiot's Fare," Manguel cite les reproches faits à Doris Lessing par son éditeur anglais: "You write too much."

Il ne s'agit pas ici de jouer les Don Quichotte contre l'environnement commercial dans lequel nous nous trouvons. Depuis longtemps déjà, l'Amérique ouvre la voie – comme Tocqueville l'affirme dès le milieu du XIXe siècle[3] – et tous les pays capitalistes lui emboîtent le pas, la globalisation ne faisant qu'accélérer ce processus. La résistance face à un phénomène de production artistique pour les masses au détriment de la qualité se situe dans la recherche de niches de qualité. Dans cette dynamique, le rôle de l'éditeur n'est plus celui que redoute Manguel ni celui que décrit Gerald Gross dans *Editors on Editing*[4].

Loin d'être réduit à un travail de simple toilettage, ce rôle n'outrepasse pas pour autant les limites d'une fonction éditoriale telle que nous l'entendons traditionnellement en France. En effet, si la création de l'œuvre reste de l'entière responsabilité de l'auteur, l'éditeur, sans en déranger le *contenu*, identifie plusieurs chantiers sur lesquels il peut apporter une contribution précieuse. Mes entretiens avec Douglas Gibson permettent de clarifier ses domaines d'interventions et je me contente ici de les résumer en quelques points. L'éditeur d'ouvrages de qualité est celui qui :

- effectue un repérage puis une sélection de manuscrits de valeur ;
- encourage l'auteur en respectant son besoin d'autonomie ;
- facilite les conditions matérielles du travail de l'auteur ;
- optimise le toilettage sans nuire à l'équilibre créatif ;

---

[3]   "La démocratie ne fait pas seulement pénétrer le goût des lettres dans les classes industrielles, elle introduit l'esprit industriel au sein de la littérature." Et : "[C]hez les nations démocratiques, un écrivain peut se flatter d'obtenir à bon marché une médiocre renommée et une grande fortune. Il n'est pas nécessaire pour cela qu'on l'admire, il suffit qu'on le goûte.

La foule toujours croissante des lecteurs et le besoin continuel qu'ils ont du nouveau assurent le débit d'un livre qu'ils n'estiment guère." Tocqueville (de), Alexis. *De la Démocratie en Amérique, tome 2*. Paris: Garnier-Flammarion, 1981, 51.

[4]   Gross, Gerald, *Editors on Editing*, New York, Grove Press, 1993. Dans ce volume, figurent plusieurs articles traitant du rôle de l'éditeur. Gerald Howard commente, par exemple: "the intersection between culture and commerce where editors do their work is … a sanguine piece of ground." Gerald Howard "Mistah Perkins – He Dead," *Editors on Editing*, New York, Grove Press, 1993, p. 58. Ce type d'éditeur décrit par Howard en arrive à ériger un modèle d'écrivain carriériste et sans vocation particulière : "Go to the right college, get into the right … program, make the right contacts among established writers and book and magazine editors, find the right literary agent, who'll sell your book to the right publisher, who'll give your book the right cover and shake down the right writers … for the right blurbs, and you're off!" *Ibidem*, p. 67.

- joue sur les paramètres éditoriaux autres que le contenu créatif (comme le *timing*) ;
- protège l'auteur contre les pièges des événements promotionnels,

et enfin et surtout, pour revenir à la genèse de l'œuvre, se propose d'être le premier lecteur de l'auteur, lui offrant par son respect de l'œuvre la confiance dont ce dernier a besoin.

Une illustration parfaite du cumul de ces fonctions nous est donnée par le texte de Douglas Gibson intitulé « Alligators in the Sewers » où l'éditeur retrace l'histoire du manuscrit *No Great Mischief.* Indépendamment du caractère divertissant de cette aventure, nous découvrons comment Douglas Gibson accompagne Alistair MacLeod dans la dernière étape de l'élaboration de son œuvre. La confiance aveugle que l'éditeur offre à son auteur (au point d'inscrire le roman au catalogue de la rentrée 1999 sans avoir lu un seul mot du manuscrit), ainsi que l'efficacité avec laquelle il gère les paramètres matériels de la publication du roman (en interne chez M&S, comme en externe), témoignent en faveur d'une pratique éditoriale qui se situe à l'opposé de l'arrogance décrite par Manguel, Gross ou Howard. Bien sûr, apparaît clairement la jubilation de pouvoir participer à l'histoire de la parution d'une grande œuvre telle que *No Great Mischief* – jubilation que Douglas Gibson invite chacun à partager, jusqu'aux deux stagiaires chargées de la frappe du manuscrit. Et cette joie est bien légitime ! Mais si Douglas Gibson peut être tenté de s'enorgueillir d'avoir réalisé pour le compte d'Alistair MacLeod un découpage du roman en chapitres, dans son introduction *No Great Mischief,* il préfère souligner que le travail qu'il a effectué ne nécessitait aucun remaniement particulier. L'évidence avec laquelle sa proposition s'est imposée semble confirmer que Douglas Gibson a agi en lecteur passionné, entièrement consacré à son exercice de lecture et soucieux par ailleurs d'offrir à son auteur la chance de « sortir » son roman à un moment judicieux du point de vue du marketing.

Pour finir, j'aimerais donc souligner la double réflexion que peut susciter cet ouvrage *Douglas Gibson Unedited* : Comme je l'ai indiqué dans mon introduction, j'invite mes collègues universitaires à se pencher sur les archives léguées par l'éditeur à l'université de McMaster. Mais au-delà de l'intérêt particulier que nous portons au travail de Douglas Gibson et de sa place privilégiée aux côtés des écrivains qui contribuent fortement à l'histoire littéraire canadienne, *Douglas Gibson Unedited* permet de soulever un certain nombre de questions sur l'évolution récente du métier d'éditeur dans le contexte actuel. L'exemple singulier de Douglas Gibson, qui constitue une forme de résistance au modèle caricatural de l'*editor*, est en effet proposé comme une piste de réflexion à tous les acteurs de la chaîne du livre pleinement conscients des pressions commerciales d'aujourd'hui, afin de construire une voie éditoriale qui permette un respect de l'œuvre malgré le contexte commercial et les structures de pouvoir établies[5].

Si je m'attache à mettre en évidence la possibilité d'une résistance contre ce double danger guettant l'éditeur aujourd'hui – céder aux pressions du marché et à l'orgueilleuse tentation du pouvoir sur l'œuvre –, je souhaite également laisser entrevoir la véritable joie que procure l'acceptation, dans l'enthousiasme et l'humilité, d'un rôle périphérique dont on ne cessera de souligner la valeur. Comme le rappelle l'éditeur de Fitzgerald et de Thomas Wolf, Maxwell Perkins, en s'adressant à ses confrères : « Ce n'est pas l'éditeur qui améliore l'ouvrage. Dans le meilleur des cas, il est au service de l'auteur. N'allez donc pas vous imaginer que vous avez de l'importance, car l'éditeur ne contribue à l'ouvrage que dans la mesure où il libère l'énergie de l'auteur. Ce n'est pas l'éditeur qui crée. »[6]

C'est dans cette philosophie fondée sur un infini respect pour l'œuvre et l'auteur que s'inscrit le travail de Douglas Gibson et celui de tout éditeur de talent.

---

[5]   Cette réflexion fait écho à l'exhortation de Gerald Howard: "Yes, the corporate Shenanigans … still go on, the agents call the tune, the culture is decaying, nobody reads anymore, the universe will eventually suffer heat death… Meanwhile, the good editor's task – and there are plenty of good editors out there… – *is simply to ignore all this* and go about the business of bringing the best books he or she can to market, at a price that makes turning a profit possible. This may mean any number of personal and business compromises with a commercial culture capable of the most stupefying inanition. But victories, however difficult to win, are the lifeblood of editors, and they come more often than what one might expect… It means that the soul of publishing, and to a certain extent of American literary and intellectual culture, if that's not too grandiose, resides in the stewardship of editors who care deeply about quality and excellence.

And so we soldier on. And so we'd better." Gerald Howard "Mistah Perkins – He Dead," *Editors on Editing*, New York, Grove Press, 1993, p. 72.

[6]   Berg, A. Scott. *Max Perkins Editor of Genius*. New York: Riverhead Books, 1978, 6.

Bibliography

Evain Christine, Khandpur Reena, eds. *Atwood on her work: "Poems open the doors. Novels are the corridors."* CRINI/CEC Canadensis series, Université de Nantes, 2006.

Gross, Gerald, ed. *Editors on Editing*. New York: Grove Press, 1993.

Guilford, Irene, ed. *Alistair MacLeod, Essays On His Works*. Toronto: Guernica Editions, 1992.

Hyde, Lewis. *The Gift*. London: Random House, 1999.

King, James. *The Story of Jack McClelland*. Toronto: Alfred A. Knopf, 1999.

Lorimer Rowland, John W. Maxwell, and Jillain G. Shoichet, eds. *Book Publishing 1: Publishing Studies*. Vancouver: CCSP, 2005.

MacSkimming, Roy. *The Perilous Trade*. Toronto: McClelland & Stewart, 2003.

———. "Making Literary History," Anansi website.

Manguel, Alberto. "Idiot's Fare" *Geist* 63, Winter 2006. pp. 63-66

———. "The Secret Sharer" in *Into the Looking-Glass Wood: Essays on Books, Reading, and the World*. Toronto: Alfred Knopf Canada, 1998. pp. 130-140.

Schriffin, Andre. *The Business of Books: How the International Conglomerates Took Over Publishing and Changed the Way We Read*. New York: Verso Books, 2000.

Spadoni, Carl and Judy Donnelly, compilers. *A Bibliography of McClelland and Stewart Imprints, 1909-1985: A Publisher's Legacy*. Toronto: ECW Press, 1993.

Skelton Grant, Judith. Letter from Robertson Davies *For Your Eye Alone*. Toronto: McClelland & Stewart, Penguin Books, 1999.

Thacker, R. 2005. *Alice Munro: Writing Her Lives: A Biography*. Toronto: McClelland & Stewart

For references of the novels and volumes of short stories by Robertson Davies, Alice Munro, W.O. Mitchell, Mavis Gallant, Jack Hodgins, Alistair MacLeod, Donald Jack and William Weintraub, see the M&S website.